Jurisprudence
2012–2013

Routledge
Taylor & Francis Group

LONDON AND NEW YORK

Seventh edition published 2012
by Routledge
2 Park Square, Milton Park, Abingdon, Oxon OX14 4RN

Simultaneously published in the USA and Canada
by Routledge
711 Third Avenue, New York, NY 10017

Routledge is an imprint of the Taylor & Francis Group, an informa business

© 2012 Routledge

First edition published by Cavendish Publishing Limited 1997
Sixth edition published by Routledge 2010

British Library Cataloguing in Publication Data
A catalogue record for this book is available from the British Library

ISBN: 978-0-415-68342-5 (pbk)
ISBN: 978-0-203-30747-2 (ebk)

Typeset in Rotis
by RefineCatch Limited, Bungay, Suffolk

Printed and bound in Great Britain by
TJ International Ltd, Padstow, Cornwall

Contents

Table of Cases

Table of Statutes

How to use this book

Welcome to this new edition of Routledge Jurisprudence Lawcards. In response to student feedback, we've added some new features to these new editions to give you all the support and preparation you need in order to face your law exams with confidence.

Inside this book you will find:

■ NEW tables of cases and statutes for ease of reference

◼ Revision Checklists

We've summarised the key topics you will need to know for your law exams and broken them down into a handy revision checklist. Check them out at the beginning of each chapter, then after you have the chapter down, revisit the checklist and tick each topic off as you gain knowledge and confidence.

1

Sources of law

Primary legislation: Acts of Parliament	◼
Secondary legislation	◼
Case law	◼
System of precedent	◼
Common law	◼
Equity	◼
EU law	◼
Human Rights Act 1998	◼

■ Key Cases

We've identified the key cases that are most likely to come up in exams. To help you to ensure that you can cite cases with ease, we've included a brief account of the case and judgment for a quick aide-memoire.

HENDY LENNOX v GRAHAME PUTTICK [1984]

Basic facts

Diesel engines were supplied, subject to a *Romalpa* clause, then fitted to generators. Each engine had a serial number. When the buyer became insolvent the seller sought to recover one engine. The Receiver argued that the process of fitting the engine to the generator passed property to the buyer. The court disagreed and allowed the seller to recover the still identifiable engine despite the fact that some hours of work would be required to disconnect it.

Relevance

If the property remains identifiable and is not irredeemably changed by the manufacturing process a *Romalpa* clause may be viable.

■ Companion Website

At the end of each chapter you will be prompted to visit the Routledge Lawcards companion website where you can test your understanding online with specially prepared multiple-choice questions, as well as revise the key terms with our online glossary.

You should now be confident that you would be able to tick all of the boxes on the checklist at the beginning of this chapter. To check your knowledge of Sources of law why not visit the companion website and take the Multiple Choice Question test. Check your understanding of the terms and vocabulary used in this chapter with the flashcard glossary.

■ Exam Practice

Once you've acquired the basic knowledge, you'll want to put it to the test. The Routledge Questions and Answers provides examples of the kinds of questions that you will face in your exams, together with suggested answer plans and a fully-worked model answer. We've included one example free at the end of this book to help you put your technique and understanding into practice.

QUESTION 1

What are the main sources of law today?

Answer plan

This is, apparently, a very straightforward question, but the temptation is to ignore the European Community (EU) as a source of law and to over-emphasise custom as a source. The following structure does not make these mistakes:

■ in the contemporary situation, it would not be improper to start with the EU as a source of UK law;

■ then attention should be moved on to domestic sources of law: statute and common law;

■ the increased use of delegated legislation should be emphasised;

■ custom should be referred to, but its extremely limited operation must be emphasised.

ANSWER

European law

Since the UK joined the European Economic Community (EEC), now the EU, it has progressively but effectively passed the power to create laws which are operative in this country to the wider European institutions. The UK is now subject to Community law, not just as a direct consequence of the various treaties of accession passed by the UK Parliament, but increasingly, it is subject to the secondary legislation generated by the various institutions of the EU.

The nature of jurisprudence

1

WHAT IS JURISPRUDENCE?

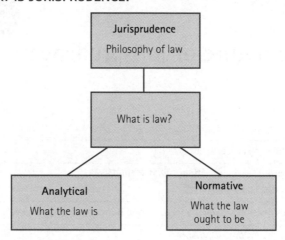

PROBLEMS OF DEFINITION

The word 'jurisprudence' is derived from two Latin words – *juris*, meaning 'of law', and *prudens*, meaning 'skilled'. The term has been used variously at different times, ranging from its use to describe mere knowledge of the law to its more specific definition as a description of the scientific investigation of fundamental legal phenomena.

A strict definition of jurisprudence is, as is the case with many general terms, difficult to articulate. The main problem with jurisprudence is that its scope of inquiry ranges over many different subjects and touches on many other disciplines, such as economics, politics, sociology and psychology, which would normally be regarded as having little to do with law and legal study.

As such, the best definition is perhaps that supplied by Roger Cotterrell in *The Politics of Jurisprudence*: 'Jurisprudence is probably best defined negatively as encompassing all kinds of general intellectual inquiries about law that are not confined solely to doctrinal exegesis or technical prescription.'

As a subject, jurisprudence may be said to involve the study of a wide range of social phenomena, with the specific aim of understanding the nature, place and role of law within society. The main question which jurisprudence seeks to answer is general and may be phrased simply as:

What is the nature of law?

This question can be seen as being actually two questions in one, that is:

What is the law?

What constitutes good law?

Answers to these two questions constitute two major divisions in jurisprudential inquiry. These are:

- descriptive or analytical jurisprudence; and

- normative jurisprudence.

These two divisions were first clearly specified by John Austin in his text *The Province of Jurisprudence Determined* (1832). Other divisions and subdivisions have been identified and argued for as the field of jurisprudence or legal philosophy has expanded.

SOME DISTINCTIONS IN JURISPRUDENCE

The work of jurists can be divided into various distinctive areas, depending mainly on the specific subject matter with which the study deals. What follow are some of the more important divisions and subdivisions, although it is important to remember that there are others.

Descriptive or analytical jurisprudence

Involves the scientific analysis of legal structures and concepts and the empirical exercise involved in discovering and elucidating the basic elements constituting law in specific legal systems. The question to be answered is: what is the law?

Normative jurisprudence

Refers to the evaluation of legal rules and legal structures on the basis of some standard of perfection and the specification of criteria for what constitutes 'good' law. This involves questions of what the law ought to be.

General jurisprudence
Refers to an abstracted study of the legal rules to be found generally in the more developed legal systems.

Particular jurisprudence
The specific analysis of the structures and other elements of a single legal system.

Historical jurisprudence
A study of the historical development and growth of legal systems and the changes involved in that growth.

Critical jurisprudence
Studies intended to provide an estimation of the real value of mainstream ideas about and theories of law with a view to providing proposals for necessary changes to such systems.

Sociological jurisprudence
Seeks to clarify the link between law and other social phenomena and to determine the extent to which its creation and operation are influenced and affected by social interests.

Economic jurisprudence
Investigates the effects on the creation and application of the law of various economic phenomena, for example, private ownership of property.

THE TERMINOLOGY OF JURISPRUDENCE

Many of the terms used in the study of jurisprudence are relatively unfamiliar and belong more to the realm of philosophy than to that of law. The following are some of the more commonly used terms and brief explanations of what they may mean in specific contexts. It is important always to remember that specific meanings are sometimes ascribed to certain terms by particular jurists, and that these meanings may be different from the ordinary usages.

Cognitivism
This is the position according to which sentences used in a given discourse are cognitive, that is, are meaningful and capable of being *true* or *false* – for example,

'grass is green' is a true proposition. In the area of jurisprudence, it refers to the view that it is possible to know the truth about things – for example, what constitutes truth about justice. Thus in the cognitivist approach the sentence 'it is always wrong to kill another human being' can be true or false.

Contractarian

This applies to assertions or assumptions that human society is based upon a social contract, whether that contract is seen as a genuine historical fact, or whether it is hypothesised as a logical presumption for the establishment and maintenance of the ties of social civility.

Dialectical

Dialectic is a debating method first used by Greek philosophers. It instrumental-ises contradiction, or the exchange of arguments and counter-arguments respectively advocating *propositions* (theses) and *counter-propositions* (antitheses). At its most simplistic, the dialectical operation can be set out in this form:

- *Thesis:* an existing or established idea.

This is challenged by an:

- *Antithesis:* an opposite and contradictory idea.

The outcome of the ensuing struggle between the thesis and the antithesis is a union and interpenetration of the two opposites, which constitutes the:

- *Synthesis:* a newer and higher form of idea, which contains qualitatively superior elements pertaining to the two opposites.

The new synthesis, however, will inevitably be challenged by another, newer and opposite idea, and so the synthesis becomes the new thesis, with its antithesis being the new opposite. The continual repetition of this cycle of struggle and resolution constitutes the dialectic, and results in development and change in all things.

Discretion

In judicial decision-making, the supposition that judges, in making decisions in 'hard cases' – that is, cases where there is no clear rule of law which is applicable or where there is an irresolvable conflict of applicable rules or again, when there is no single right answer to a legal problem – make decisions which are based on their own personal and individual conceptions of right and wrong, or what is best in terms of public policy or social interest, and that in so deciding they are exercising a quasi-legislative function and creating new law.

Many positivists, for example, John Austin and Herbert Hart, would allow for the fact that where there is no clearly applicable rule of law judges do in fact exercise their discretion in deciding cases. Ronald Dworkin, however, strongly denies this and argues that judges have no discretion in 'hard cases' and that in every case there is always a 'right answer' to the question of who has a right to win.

Efficacy

Effectiveness and efficiency, as in the capacity of a certain measure, structure or process to achieve a particular, desired result.

For Hans Kelsen, efficacy is a specific requirement for the existence of a legal system and therefore of law, as in the capacity of officials to apply sanctions regularly and efficiently in certain situations.

Empiricism

In legal philosophy, an approach to legal theory which rejects all judgments of value and regards only those statements which can be objectively verifiable as being true propositions about the nature of law. Legal empiricism is based upon an inductive process of reasoning, requiring the empirical observation of facts and the formulation of a hypothesis which is then applied to the facts, before an explanatory theory of legal phenomena can be postulated.

Formalism

In legal theory, the approach which seeks to minimise the element of choice in the interpretation of terms contained in legal rules and emphasises the necessity of certainty and predictability in the meaning of such rules. Legal formalists would advocate the attribution of specific meanings to certain terms from which the interpreter of a legal rule could not deviate, and require that such terms should have those same meanings in every case where the rule is applicable. Formalism is to be contrasted with Realism.

Functionalism

For functionalism, society is made up of interdependent sections which combine to fulfil the functions necessary for the survival of society as a whole. A functionalist interpretation of the law will therefore focus on the social functions fulfilled by law.

Good
Some value or interest which it is generally considered desirable to attain or provide for in social arrangements, for example, liberty, equality or dignity.

Imperative
With reference to theoretical approaches to the nature of law, the conception which regards law as being constituted generally by the commands, orders or coercive actions of a specific, powerful person or body of persons in society. The main imperative theories are the positivist approaches of:

- *Bentham* and *Austin*: law as a set of general commands of a sovereign backed by the threat of sanctions;

- *Kelsen*: law as a system of conditional directives (primary norms) to officials to apply sanctions.

Intuitionism
Intuition is the immediate apprehension of an object by the mind without the intervention of any reasoning process. Intuitionism refers to the view in moral philosophy according to which humans possess a faculty, conscience, by which they are able directly to discover and determine what is morally right or wrong, good or evil.

Justice
In its jurisprudential use justice refers to fairness at the aggregate level of society as opposed to fairness to the individual. In this sense the ideal of justice can be contrasted to the human rights discourse.

Libertarian
Of or concerning approaches to legal and social arrangements which generally give priority to the concept of liberty, or the specification, attainment and protection of particular basic freedoms.

Materialism
In Marxist theory, the notion that changes and developments in human society are based on the material conditions of human existence. The two notions of dialectical materialism and historical materialism in Marxist theory are based on

the assumption that there are ongoing associations and contradictions between various social, technical, economic and political phenomena which determine the historical development of society.

Morality
The making, holding or expression of moral judgments, that is, conceptions of what is good and bad, right and wrong or acceptable and unacceptable as judged in accordance with some standard which may be a personal or social convention.

Moral philosophy
The formalised attempt to understand the thinking underlying or reinforcing moral judgments.

Realism
For legal realists all law is made by human beings and is therefore imperfect. Law is intrinsically concerned with the practical outcomes of cases. The law is not neutral and objective but reflects political, social, and psychological processes at work beneath the surface of formal legal reasoning. Realists study law empirically, in practice and in context, and not as a formal system of rules.

TWO APPROACHES TO MORAL PHILOSOPHY

There are two main approaches to moral philosophy which comprise distinct theoretical schools of thought.

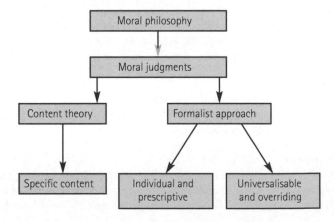

(1) FORMALIST APPROACHES

These argue generally that what constitutes morality is entirely a question of personal value judgments – morality is a question of the attitude which a person has to a particular issue or problem, rather than an intrinsic quality of the issue or problem itself. Morality cannot therefore be made the subject of empirical and objective observation and analysis, and thus there is no theoretically defensible answer as to what morality is. Moral philosophy should, therefore, be concerned with purely formal questions. In this regard, a moral judgment may be identified by having regard to four formal characteristics.

(i) Prescriptive

It must constitute a specific recommendation, directed at oneself and others as to how to act in certain circumstances.

(ii) Overriding

It must be intended that where there is a conflict between the moral judgment in question and any other recommendations, then the former must take precedence.

(iii) Universalisable

The recommendation that a moral judgment must be capable of applying, and intended to apply, not only to the issue or problem in hand but also to all similar cases.

(iv) Categorical

It is not hostage to the personal ends of the subject who carries out the judgment.

Note: the formalist approach is best expressed in Immanuel Kant's moral philosophy. Kant formulated the categorical imperative as follows in *Groundwork of the Metaphysics of Morals*: 'Act only according to that maxim whereby you can at the same time will that it should become a universal law.' Thus, for example, according to the categorical imperative, lying is always immoral, even if one lies to save the life of a friend.

(2) CONTENT THEORIES

These regard morality as something which has or can have a specific content and which, therefore, can be objectively identified and empirically analysed. Morality constitutes a definite social phenomenon which has developed to assist mankind in dealing with recurring problems of the human condition. It comprises principles for establishing the proper balance in the interrelation-ships between persons in society and for protecting interests and values which are regarded as being vital in various societies. Law can, therefore, be consid-ered invalid if it substantially deviates from the requirements of such principles. An example of this approach to morality is Thomas Aquinas' view that '*lex injusta non est lex sed corruptio legis*' (an unjust law is not law).

Natural law

The philosophy of law which proceeds from an assumption that law is a social necessity based on the moral perceptions of rational persons and that any law which violates certain moral codes is not valid at all. Human law is thus based on certain universal principles, discoverable through reason or revelation, which are seen as being eternal, immutable, and ultimately based on the nature of human beings.

Norm

A generally accepted standard of social behaviour. Note that Hans Kelsen uses the term in his definition of law as 'the primary norm that stipulates the sanc-tion' to refer specifically to 'a conditional directive given to officials to apply sanctions under certain circumstances'.

Obligation

For Herbert Hart, a distinction must be made between 'being obliged' to act or forbear, and being 'under an obligation' to act or forbear, the former being moti-vated by fear of some sanction which occurs as an external stimulus, and the latter being comprised of both the external element and an internal element whereby the subject feels a sense of duty to act or forbear.

Policy

A statement of a social or community goal aimed at some improvement of the social, economic or political welfare of the members of the group in general. As such, a policy may be pursued sometimes even though this would lead to a restriction of the rights of individuals. Dworkin makes a specific distinction between matters of policy as defined and matters of principle, which he regards as setting out the rights of individuals, and he points out the need for justice and fairness in creating a balance between the two.

Positivism

The approach to the study of law which considers the only valid laws to be those laws that have been 'posited', that is, created and put forward by human beings in positions of power in society. Generally, positivism rejects the attempt of Natural Law theory to link law to morality. Herbert Hart has identified at least six different ways in which the term 'positivism' may be employed:

1 Positivism in the definition of law: that law in the wider sense is defined as the expression of human will and that law as the command of the 'sovereign' is the most prominent example of this form of positivism.

2 Positivism as a theory of a form of legal study: the object of which is the analysis or clarification of the meanings of legal concepts, that is, analytical jurisprudence, which is purely a conceptual – as distinct from a sociological, historical, political or moral – investigation of the law.

3 Positivism as a theory of the judicial process: that a legal system is a closed logical system in which correct decisions can be deduced from a conjunction of a statement of the relevant legal rules and a statement about the facts of the case.

4 Positivism as a theory of law and morals: that there is no necessary connection between law as it is and law as it ought to be, the so called 'separation thesis'.

5 Positivism and non-cognitivism in ethics: that moral judgments cannot be established by rational argument, evidence or proof.

6 Positivism and identification of a valid law: if valid, then there is an unconditional obligation to obey the law, no matter what the content.

Principle

As opposed to a policy, a statement or proposition which describes the rights which individuals may hold apart from those which are specified in the legal rules of a community.

Rationality

The ability to use one's reason or mental faculties generally to evaluate alternative courses of action, to make choices in terms of one's preferences, to set goals and to formulate efficient plans for the attainment of such goals.

Realism

The philosophical approach which emphasises objectivity over sentiment and idealism in the investigation of phenomena. Realists generally argue that the perception of phenomena is an experience of objective things which are independent of the private sense-data that we may initially hold. A meaningful analysis of the nature of law must therefore concentrate on the objective experience of the actual practice of the courts, rather than on some 'rules' which are supposed to guide the attitudes of judicial officials. Legal realism has expressed itself in two main forms:

1 *Scandinavian realism*: espoused by Hagerstrom (1868–1939), Lundstedt (1882–1955), Olivecrona (1897–1980) and Ross (1899–1979). This movement generally rejects metaphysical speculation on the nature of law, regards the ideas and principles of Natural Law as being unacceptable, and argues that the only meaningful propositions about law are those which can be verified through the experience of the senses.

2 *American realism*: William James (1890–1922), John Dewey (1859–1952) and other jurists of this school emphasised the actual practice of the courts and the decisions of judges as comprising the essential elements of law. The law, they argued, is not to be found in certain rules and concepts which may guide officials to reach decisions. It is rather to be found in the actual decisions of judges and predictions of these; for, until a judge pronounces what he or she is going to do about a particular case, we can never know what the law is going to be and how it is going to be applied. Such things as statutes, for example, are therefore merely sources of the law rather than a part of the law itself.

Rule

A statement formally specifying a required mode or standard of behaviour. Note: Herbert Hart, in *The Concept of Law* (1961), emphasises the nature of a rule as a generally accepted standard of behaviour. Law is then constituted by a systemic interaction between specific types of social rules with particular characteristics: primary rules, which impose duties on citizens to act or forbear in certain situations; and secondary rules which are power-conferring and which determine how the primary rules may be properly created, applied and changed (see later discussion of the contrast between rules and principles, Chapter 4).

Sanction

The formal consequence (usually negative or harmful) which is directed at, and normally follows from a specific act of a particular person or persons, where that act is regarded by society or some specific organ of society, for example, the State, as being a requisite condition for the consequence and a justification for the exertion by society or the State of some of its legitimate power against the person or persons.

Note: John Austin, in *The Province of Jurisprudence Determined* (1832), defines sanctions negatively as constituting some 'harm, pain or evil'. He regards sanctions as being a necessary element of law since, for him, the law is made up of the general commands (that is, the expression of certain wishes) of a sovereign, backed by sanctions – that is, the threat of some negative consequences which may follow from non-compliance with the command by the sovereign's subjects. Hans Kelsen, in *General Theory of Law and the State* (1945), regards sanctions both positively and negatively as constituting either punishments or rewards which officials are directed to mete out to citizens under certain conditions. For Kelsen, sanctions are also an essential element of law, since all law in fact comprises 'primary norms' or conditional directives to officials to apply sanctions under certain circumstances.

Social constructionism

A sociological theory of knowledge which considers how social phenomena develop in particular social contexts. A social construct, even though it may seem self-evident to the participants of a given society, is in fact the invention of that society.

Teleology

The view that everything has an ultimate end or purpose towards which it will inevitably develop. Classical Natural Law theorists would argue, for example, that humans and their society have as an end some ultimate state of perfection, to which they must naturally approximate and towards which they must necessarily strive, and that law is an essential device for precipitating this end (from the Greek *telos*, meaning end, purpose).

Utilitarianism

The approach of moral philosophy which regards an act, measure or social or legal arrangement as being good or just if its overall effect is to advance the happiness or general welfare of the majority of persons in society. Utilitarianism is a goal-based approach to the problems of justice in the distribution of the benefits and burdens of society, in that it gives precedence to the advancement of the collective good or welfare, even if this may involve extinguishing or curtailing the rights and political or other liberties of the individual.

BRANCHES OF UTILITARIAN THEORY

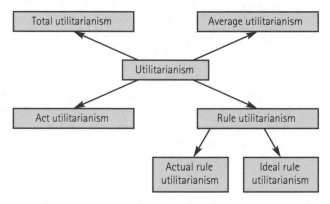

- ◼ **Total (classical) utilitarianism**: where social and legal measures or institutions are regarded as just if their operation, on the whole, serves to maximise aggregate happiness or welfare.

- ◼ **Average utilitarianism**: where social and legal measures or institutions are regarded as just if their operation, on the whole, serves to maximise average happiness or welfare *per capita*.

- ◼ **Act utilitarianism**: where a specific act or measure is regarded as right if it will on the whole have the best consequences.

- **Actual rule utilitarianism**: where an act or measure is regarded as right if it is permitted by a rule which, if generally followed, will on the whole have the best consequences.

- **Ideal rule utilitarianism**: where an act or measure is regarded as being right if it is permitted by a rule which, if generally followed, will on the whole have consequences as good as or better than any other rule governing the same act.

THE SUBJECT MATTER OF JURISPRUDENCE

WHAT IS INVOLVED IN THE STUDY OF JURISPRUDENCE?

The broad divisions of jurisprudential inquiry have been set out above. Those divisions clearly illustrate that jurisprudence covers a wide area of study, dealing with a variety of issues and topics as well as touching on a whole range of other disciplines such as philosophy, political science, sociology, religious studies, economics. What brings unity to jurisprudence as a field of study, however, is that all lines of inquiry revolve around the same two questions:

What is law?

What ought the law to be?

Indeed all jurisprudential currents essentially seek to explain the incidence, existence and consequence of law as a social phenomenon, and to criticise it constructively. Consequently, the questions that tend to be asked have to do with the following matters:

- the origin and sources of law generally and/or in specific societies;

- the historical development of law in general and the emergence and evolution of specific legal systems, traditions and practices;

- the meaning of specific legal concepts and the construction of various legal structures and processes;

- the link between law and other social phenomena such as political ideologies, economic interests, social classes, and moral and religious conventions;

■ the operation of the law as a mode of social control, and the effects that it has on the persons to whom it applies in terms of justice as well as social, economic and political developments.

You should now be confident that you would be able to tick all the boxes on the checklist at the beginning of this chapter. To check your knowledge of The nature of jurisprudence why not visit the companion website and take the Multiple Choice Question test. Check your understanding of the terms and vocabulary used in this chapter with the flashcard glossary.

2

Natural law theory

THE ESSENCE OF NATURAL LAW THEORY

Natural Law theory seeks to explain law as a phenomenon which is based upon and which ought to approximate to some higher law contained in certain principles of morality. These principles find their source in either religion or reason. This chapter deals with classical natural law theories while Chapter 4 deals with Dworkin and anti-positivistic theories.

TWO MAIN APPROACHES OF NATURAL LAW THEORY

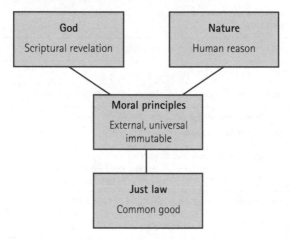

Theological theories

These regard the universe and human society as being under the governance of some Deity, who has laid down constant principles which must eternally control all of creation. These principles constitute a higher law which is universal, that is, common to all societies, and immutable, that is, it cannot be changed through human agency. This higher law can be grasped through Revelation as in the scriptures or through the use of Reason. All human arrangements, including law, must conform as far as is possible to these principles.

Secular theories

These proceed from regarding human beings as having a certain conception of morality which is intrinsic to them and to their nature. This morality, which sometimes manifests itself in the form of conscience, is made up of basic principles which form a basis for proper human action. These principles are discoverable through the application of Reason and they ought to form the proper basis for law making. To this extent they constitute a 'higher law' to which all human laws must strive to conform.

FIVE PRESUPPOSITIONS OF NATURAL LAW THEORY

1 Natural Law is based on value judgments which emanate from some absolute source and which are in accordance with Nature and Reason.
2 These value judgments express objectively ascertainable principles which govern the essential nature of persons and of the universe.
3 The principles of Natural Law are immutable, eternally valid and can be grasped by the proper employment of human reason.
4 These principles are universal and when grasped they must overrule all positive law, which will not truly be law unless it conforms to Natural Law.
5 Law is a fundamental requirement of human life in society.

THE GENERAL METHODOLOGY OF NATURAL LAW THEORY

Natural Law theorists have a teleological view of the universe and of human society. This means that they regard the world, especially human society, as having an ultimate purpose which generally refers to some state of perfection towards which society is advancing.

Law, as a device for promoting the desired good, is regarded as being a social necessity in the sense that it provides both a guide for those who are working for the common good, and a control for those who may deviate from what is morally acceptable.

All human laws, if they are to be good and therefore valid, must be created in line with specific moral constraints and must operate in such a way that they provide the optimum conditions, resources and opportunities for the attainment of the common good.

The important question concerning the nature of law is therefore not what the law is at any point in time, since this may not be a true reflection of the principles of Natural Law, but what the law ought to be in order for it to be a true reflection of such principles.

A law which substantially deviates from the principles of Natural Law is not only a bad law, but can be regarded as invalid as well, since it does not truly reflect the model of what law ought to be.

THE HISTORICAL DEVELOPMENT OF NATURAL LAW THEORY

The concept of natural law was very important in the development of the common law. Parliament often made reference to the Fundamental Laws of England which were at times said to embody natural law principles and set limits on the power of the monarchy.

See diagram on facing page.

EARLY BEGINNINGS

It is possible to trace Natural Law thinking from the most primitive stages of social development when, for many simple societies, there was at some stage very little distinction made between the religious and the secular, the spiritual and the physical. Many early communities all over the world tended to see a link between the natural world of physical matter and the spiritual world of gods and spirits. The spiritual world was seen as being in control of the physical, including human society, and with a multiplicity of gods and spirits, there was a spiritual entity associated with the workings of almost every aspect of the physical world.

THE HISTORICAL DEVELOPMENT OF NATURAL LAW THEORY

This gave birth to the notion that there was some higher power in control of human existence, and therefore some higher set of rules, principles or laws which humankind could discover and utilise for the proper governance of their lives and thus lead a perfect existence.

This state of perfection was then seen as a goal which the various gods and spirits might have intended for humanity, and it thus became an ultimate purpose for all to work at achieving.

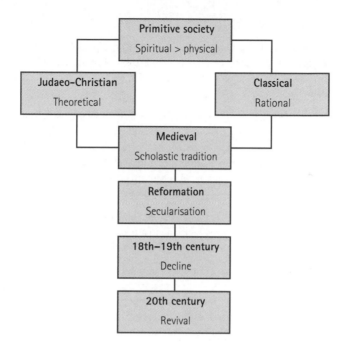

THE CLASSICAL PERIOD AND THE CHRISTIAN ERA

In Europe, the ascendancy of the Judaeo-Christian tradition replaced the poly-theism of the ancients with a monotheism which attributed the creation, governance and ultimate judgment of human society to a single Deity. It was then possible to define a singular purpose for human existence, with a divine lawgiver providing basic principles for human morality and law through the scriptures, and requiring that societies govern themselves on the basis of these principles.

Parallel to this spiritual/religious development of Natural Law, early Greek and pre-Socratic philosophers developed the idea of rationalism. They surmised that the universe was governed by intelligible laws capable of being grasped by the human mind. It was therefore possible to derive, from the rationality of the universe, rational principles which could be utilised to govern life in society.

Some examples of classical Natural Law thinking are:

- *Socrates* (470–399 BCE) argued that there were principles of morality which it was possible to discover through the processes of reasoning and insight. Law based on these principles would thus be the product of correct reasoning.

- *Plato* (428–348 BCE) further developed the 'idea' of justice as an absolute 'thing-in-itself' having qualities of truth and reality higher than those of positive law, which could then be seen as a mere shadow of real justice. Law must constantly strive to approximate to the Absolute Idea of justice, and ideal justice could only be achieved or fully realised in an ideal State ruled over by philosopher-kings capable of grasping the Absolute Idea of justice.

- *Aristotle* (384–322 BCE) recognised Nature as the capacity for development inherent in particular things, aimed at a particular end or purpose, in both physical and moral phenomena. He also made a distinction between:

  - *Natural justice*: common to all humankind and based on the fundamental end or purpose of human beings as social and political beings, which he concluded to be the attainment of a 'state of goodness';
  - *Conventional justice*: varies from State to State in accordance with the history and needs of particular human communities.

- The *Stoics* identified Nature with Reason, arguing that Reason governs all parts of the universe, and that humans, as part of the universe and of Nature, are also governed by Reason. People will therefore live 'naturally' if they lived according to their Reason.

- *Cicero* (106–43 BCE) argued that Nature provided rules by which humankind ought to live and that these rules, which could be discovered through Reason, should form the basis of all law. He established the view that an unjust law is not law and argued that a test of good law was whether it accorded with the dictates of Nature.

THE MEDIEVAL PERIOD

This stage in European history saw the final integration of the rationalist and the religious approaches to Natural Law. Mainly this was the work of Thomas Aquinas (1224–74).

AQUINAS' FOUR CATEGORIES OF LAW

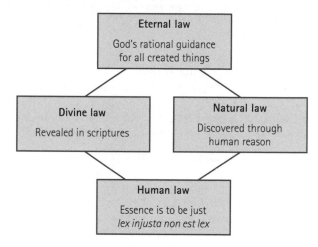

Aquinas divided law into four categories (see above):

◼ *Eternal law*: which constitutes God's rational guidance of all created things, is derived from the divine wisdom and based on a divine plan.

◼ *Divine law*: that part of eternal law which is manifested through revelations in the Christian scriptures.

◼ *Natural law*: which describes the participation of rational creatures in the eternal law through the operation of reason.

◼ *Human law*: which is derived from both Divine law and Natural law and which is, or must be, directed towards the attainment of the common good. This law may be variable in accordance with the time and circumstances in which it is formulated, but its essence is to be just. Thus: *lex injusta non est lex* (an unjust law is not law).

For Aquinas, a human law is unjust where it:

◼ furthers the interests of the lawgiver only;

◼ exceeds the powers of the lawgiver;

◼ imposes burdens unequally on the governed.

Under these circumstances, then, disobedience to an unjust law becomes a duty. However, such disobedience, though justified, should be avoided where its effects would be to lead to social instability, which is a greater evil than the existence of an unjust law.

THE SECULARISATION OF NATURAL LAW

This began with the decline of the Roman Catholic Church, following the Reformation in Europe. Essentially, this secularisation resulted from Protestant theorists seeking to develop a doctrine of Natural Law which would not be dependent on the papacy and papal pronouncements for its coherence.

One of the main secular Natural Law theorists at this stage was Hugo Grotius, a Dutch statesman and jurist who in his writings sought to separate Natural Law from its narrow theological foundations. Instead, Grotius emphasised the classical explanation of Natural Law as being grounded in the authority of Reason based on the Aristotelian system – that is, that Natural Law principles are derived or derivable from the nature of the human intellect which requires and desires society to be peaceful. Thus, these principles are independent of Divine command and it is possible to have Natural Law without appealing to God. Any law contrary to the principles so derived would be invalid from the point of view of rationality, and laws could be seen as having a constructive and practical function – the creation and maintenance of a peaceful society.

THE DECLINE OF NATURAL LAW THEORY

The 18th and 19th centuries saw the decline of Natural Law theory as it came under attack from rationalist and increasingly secularist approaches to the problems of the human condition.

THE 18TH CENTURY

In the 'age of reason', thinkers like Montesquieu (1689–1755), Hume (1711–76) and Adam Smith (1723–90) criticised Natural Law theory for its assertion that there was some ultimate, metaphysical purpose to human existence and human society separate from the moral and physical realities of everyday life.

Hume especially attacked the *a priori* reasoning behind most Natural Law thought, especially what he regarded as being the irrational attempt to derive *ought* propositions from *is* propositions.

THE 19TH CENTURY

This period saw an even more virulent attack on Natural Law theory, as emphasis was placed on the notions of State power and State coercion. For example, the German philosopher Hegel sought to deify the State which he regarded as an end-in-itself, an absolute sovereign whose essence derived from the laws of history and was therefore not subject to some external, higher law.

However, some commentators argue that although Hegel was opposed to classical conceptions of natural law, which for him were merely rationalisations *ex post facto* of the antagonism between what *is* and what *ought* to be, he introduced a much more convincing substitute for natural law with the idea of ethical life. For Hegel, true philosophy was to overcome the antagonism between *is* and *ought* in the process of actualisation of human will under the form of the ethical State. The ethical State is the realisation of *free*, or *ethical*, will. This is because for Hegel, the end of history is to actualise the ideal so there eventually should no longer be a distinction between *is* and *ought*; they would be as one. So even though this is not natural law in the classical sense, Hegel is far from being a positivist. In fact, his conception of morality is much more radical than that of traditional jusnaturalists.

The 19th century also saw the rise of the positivist approaches to law, as expounded by such theorists as Jeremy Bentham and John Austin, which sought to place a strict separation between the two notions of what the law is and what it ought to be. Law and morality could and indeed should be kept separate, and the principles of Natural Law were regarded as belonging more to the realm of morality than to that of law.

THE 20TH-CENTURY REVIVAL OF NATURAL LAW THEORY

The 20th century saw a revival of Natural Law approaches to the study of law, particularly the notion that there must be a higher set of principles, separate from the positive law, which the latter must satisfy if it is to be regarded as valid law. This revival was the result of a number of factors, including:

- the general decline of social and economic stability worldwide;

- Nazi Germany, whose acts were lawful on the basis of Nazi laws;

- the expansion of governmental activity, especially the increasing encroachment of State institutions on the private lives of citizens through the medium of the law;

■ the development of weapons of mass destruction and their increasing use in wars on a global scale;

■ increasing doubts regarding the use and effectiveness of the empirical sciences in determining and resolving problems of the human condition.

JM FINNIS AND THE RESTATEMENT OF NATURAL LAW

John Finnis, an Oxford philosopher, starts by refuting the criticism, first aired by David Hume, that classical Natural Law theory irrationally sought to derive an 'ought' from an 'is', that is, to derive normative values by reasoning from observed natural facts. He concedes that some Natural Lawyers of the classical school, especially the Stoics and the medieval rationalists, may have done so. However, he grounds his own restatement of Natural Law on the writings of Aristotle and Aquinas, whom he claims were not guilty of this irrationality.

In his reinterpretation of the writings of Aquinas, Finnis argues that the normative conclusions of Natural Law are not based on observation of human or any other nature. Rather they result from a reflective grasp of what is self-evidently good for all human beings and from a practical understanding gained by experiencing one's own nature and personal inclinations. This is Finnis' main contribution to the Natural Law debate: his substitution of intuition for rational speculation as a way to derive the 'ought' from the 'is'.

Finnis argues that objective knowledge of what is right is made possible by the existence of what he calls 'basic forms of human flourishing' which are objective 'goods' distinct from any moral evaluations of goodness. These are generally things which for most people make life worthwhile and they are self evident – that is, they would be 'obvious to anyone acquainted with the range of human opportunities'.

Natural Law, then, is a set of principles of practical reasonableness to be utilised in the ordering of human life and human community – in the process of creating optimum conditions for humans to attain the objective goods. These conditions constitute the 'common good'.

Finnis lists seven objective goods which he regards as being irreducibly basic. These are:

1 life – the first basic value;
2 knowledge – a preference for true over false belief;
3 play – performance for the sake of it;
4 aesthetic experience – the appreciation of beauty;
5 friendship or sociability – acting for the sake of one's friends' purpose or well being;
6 practical reasonableness – the use of one's intelligence to choose actions, lifestyle, character, etc;
7 religion – the ability to reflect on the origins of the cosmic order and human freedom and reason.

These objective goods are attainable only in a community of human beings where there is a legal system which facilitates the common good. Rulers have the authority to work for the common good, and unjust laws which work against the common good may be valid but they do not accord with the ruler's authority. The position of rulers may give the rules which they create a presumptive authority, but those that are unjust, though they may be technically valid, will be no more than the corruption of law.

DERYCK BEYLEVELD AND ROGER BROWNSWORD'S SECULAR NATURAL LAW THEORY

In *Law as a Moral Judgement*, Beyleveld and Brownsword put forward a Natural Law (or idealist, as they would say) theory of law that draws on the work of Immanuel Kant and Alan Gewirth.[1] While Beyleveld and Brownsword defend a Natural Law view their approach differs radically from the ones put forward by

[1] *Immanuel Kant* (1724–1804) is a central figure in the history of modern philosophy. He defends a moral theory centred on the idea of reason and autonomy. In his view, human beings should be conceived primarily as rational beings carrying an intrinsic value. As a result, no act can be considered moral if it denies the autonomy of other human beings because in so doing it contradicts the non-instrumental value of humanity.

Alan Gewirth (1912–2004) was an American philosopher who argued for the view that ethics can be founded on reason and are ultimately shaped by a supreme principle, i.e. the Principle of Generic Consistency according to which all agents have inalienable rights to the capacities and facilities they need in order to be able to act. In this way, he also provided a rational justification for human rights by connecting the notion of human right to the very possibility of human agency.

Finnis, among others, as the former, but not the latter, is secular, i.e. it stands even though we do not assume the existence of God. Further, Beyleveld and Brownsword do not endorse the idea, which has underlined the traditional forms of Natural Law theory, that there exists a higher law, namely a law independent of human acts and prescribing the basic principles that any human law ought to conform with in order to be valid law.

From the outset, Beyleveld and Brownsword make it clear that the very notion of Natural Law theory should be redefined. On their view, the defining and fundamental tenet of any Natural Law theory, as opposed to a positivist theory, is the claim that law is a moral concept: law necessarily depends on social facts as well as moral values. They thus support the 'connection thesis', meaning the view that morality impinges on law in that there obtains a (conceptually) necessary connection between law and morality. Accordingly, for Beyleveld and Brownsword legal rules ought to be consistent with some moral requirement.

To argue for this view, Beyleveld and Brownsword put forward a sophisticated argument showing that the sphere of action is ultimately governed by a supreme moral principle. This principle, which is called 'Principle of Generic Consistency' (hereafter PGC), states that necessary agents, i.e. those beings who can act for a purpose and so perform voluntary and intentional acts, must act in accord with the right of freedom of other agents as well as their own one. The PGC is the basic principle governing human behaviour and has to be accounted for by any institution that purports to order human relationships. As a result, no institution purporting to govern human conduct is entitled to incorporate norms inconsistent with the PGC. This entails that so long as law can be defined as a body of norms aiming at ordering and governing human relationships, it cannot incorporate norms contrary to the PGC, i.e. norms inconsistent with a particular moral principle. Then, it is argued, there is a necessary, or conceptual, connection between law and morality in that law cannot disregard, at the very least, a moral principle, namely the PGC.

To sum up, Beyleveld and Brownsword claim that:

1 there is a basic moral principle governing human purposive actions, the PGC;
2 law is an institution that aims at governing human purposive actions;
3 law cannot contradict the PGC or the basic principles of a morality grounded on the PGC;

4 then, it is demonstrated that there is a necessary connection between law and morals.

The implications of this argument are developed in detail by Beyleveld and Brownsword who in so doing defend an original Natural Law theory addressing important issues such as the nature of legal systems, the status of international law, the problem of political obligation, the features of legal reasoning, the legitimacy of political authority, and the role of a Constitution within a legal framework, etc. In this way, Beyleveld and Brownsword advance a comprehensive alternative to legal positivism.

THE MAIN CRITICISMS OF NATURAL LAW THEORY

Many of these have been articulated by the followers of the positivist school of thought and can be summarised as follows:

- The attempt by Natural Law theorists to derive *ought* propositions from *is* propositions is neither logically possible nor defensible. It is referred to as a 'naturalistic fallacy'.

- Natural lawyers are wrong to place a strong connection between law and morality. Although law may sometimes reflect morality, the two are distinct phenomena and should be recognised as such. An analysis of the one should therefore not impinge upon our conception of the other. A law can be valid because it has been created validly, even though it may offend our moral sensibilities.

- Morality is a matter of personal value judgments, which may change erratically for a variety of reasons. It is therefore undesirable to base the development of law, with its necessary requirement for certainty and predictability, on moral considerations as the Natural lawyers would have us do.

- The appeal by some Natural Law theorists to the existence of a 'higher law' which should be a measure of moral and legal propriety is an appeal to irrationality, since it is not possible objectively to demonstrate the existence of such principles.

You should now be confident that you would be able to tick all the boxes on the checklist at the beginning of this chapter. To check your knowledge of Natural law theory why not visit the companion website and take the Multiple Choice Question test. Check your understanding of the terms and vocabulary used in this chapter with the flashcard glossary.

Positivist theories of law

3

WHAT IS THE POSITIVIST APPROACH TO LAW?

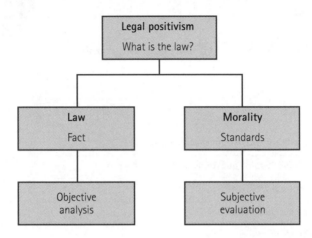

Legal positivism draws a sharp distinction between the law that 'is' and the law that 'ought' to be, which does not mean that the 'ought' question is not being addressed by legal positivists, but that it is addressed separately from the 'is' question.

According to Margaret Davies in *Asking the Law Question*: 'the idea behind "positivism" as a legal philosophy is that legal systems are "posited", that is, *created*, by people, rather than having a natural or metaphysical existence.'

Consequently, legal positivism regards the law's most important feature as being the fact that it is 'posited' by certain persons in society who are in positions of power and who provide the sole source of the validity and authority of such law. The point of legal positivism is to come to an understanding about the nature of legal systems rather than speculate about the morality of a given system. As such, the issue raised by the question: *what is law?* is essentially a question of fact, to be answered by empirical reference to, and an analysis of, objective social phenomena. Law is law if it has been created in the correct way.

In making such an analysis, only such material as can be factually identified as being legally relevant should be taken into account, because the law is a distinct phenomenon which can originate, exist and be explicable only within its own terms, even though it may have some similarities or connections with other social phenomena such as morality, religion, ethics and so on. Positivism artificially isolates the study of law from all other considerations.

An investigation into the nature of law can be seen as an attempt to answer two questions, which may in themselves be seen as elements of the general question: *what is law?* These two sub-questions can be phrased as follows.

■ **What is the law?** This is a question of fact involving an attempt to explain the actual incidence of law in various societies and to identify and analyse its basic characteristics, structures, procedures and underlying concepts and principles. In legal theory, this is normally referred to as the 'is' question, since it requires mainly the factual identification of law.

■ **What is good law?** This is a normative question requiring an evaluation of the existing law and its assessment as either good or bad by reference to some standard which specifies a goal that is regarded as being desirable and towards which good law must aspire. This, in legal theory, is generally referred to as the '*ought*' question, since it involves an assessment of the existing law in terms of whether or not it is what it ought to be by reference to the desired goal and the accepted standard of good law.

Generally, legal positivists argue that although these two questions may be equally important and deal with the same phenomenon – law – they are essentially different, deal with different issues and require different answers. They should therefore be answered separately and the issues which they involve should not be confused. Legal theorists should avoid the logical confusion which may lead them to try and derive an *ought* from an *is*. This, most legal positivists believe, has always been the problem plaguing the theories of Natural Law.

■ Being a positivist, however, does not mean that a theorist necessarily rejects the importance of certain value judgments which may be made about the law. The basic argument of positivists is that the issues of fact concerning the existence, validity and authority of law, and the issues of evaluation of such law in terms of its adequacy and propriety on the basis of some standard must be kept separate and questions relating to them must be answered separately.

■ Legal positivists normally seek to provide a formula which can be used to identify law either generally or in specific societies and systems. Most positivists believe that it is possible to provide a neutral and universally acceptable device by which investigation into the nature of law may be carried out.

THE IMPERATIVE THEORIES OF LAW

The term 'imperative' is used here to describe a particular approach of certain positivist theorists who, in their conceptions of law, emphasise the coercive element of the law and argue that law is essentially a matter of force and the imposition of sanctions by the State.

JEREMY BENTHAM (1748–1832)

See figure on facing page.

THE ORIGINS OF THE COMMAND THEORY OF LAW

Jeremy Bentham is generally credited with being the founder of the systematic imperative approach to law, although most of what he wrote in this regard was not in fact published until almost a century after his death. Bentham rejected the Natural Law approach which contended that laws were either valid or invalid depending on their goodness or badness as judged on the basis of some higher law. He did not believe in the notion of natural rights, which he described as 'nonsense on stilts'. For Bentham, only happiness was the greatest good. The 'art of legislation' consisted in the ability best to tell or predict that which would maximise happiness and minimise misery in society. The 'science of legislation', on the other hand, comprised the adequate and effective creation of laws which would advance or promote social happiness or pleasure, whilst at the same time reducing social pain and misery.

THE NATURE OF LAW

Bentham made a distinction between what he called 'expositional jurisprudence', which is the attempt to answer the factual question, *what is the law?*, and 'censorial jurisprudence', which involves the normative question of what the law ought to be, that is, *what is good law?* Bentham's answer to the first

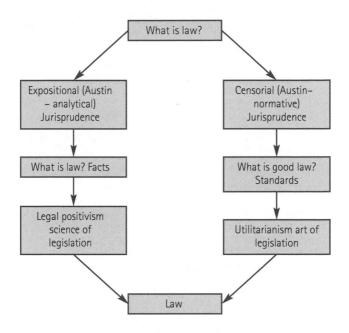

question was a positivist one, for he believed that law could only be identified and described in terms of legally relevant facts. The second question could be answered from the point of view of utility – the maximisation of pleasure and the minimisation of pain – but this answer would only be provided separately and after the requirements of the first question had been thoroughly investigated and specified.

Bentham advocated a definition of law which hinged upon the concepts of sovereignty, power and sanctions in a political society. This definition required that regard must be had to the law's:

(a) *source*: the person or persons who had created the law and whose will it is that the law expresses;

(b) *subjects*: the person or things to which the law does or may apply;

(c) *objects*: the acts, as characterised by the circumstances, to which it may apply;

(d) *extent*: the range of its application, in terms of the persons whose conduct it is intended to regulate;

(e) *aspects*: the various ways in which the will of the sovereign as expressed in the law may apply to the objects [as in (c) above] of that law;

(f) *force*: the punishments and sanctions which the law relies upon for compliance with its requirements, including such other laws and devices – what Bentham calls 'corroborative appendages' – as may be used to bring such sanctions to bear on the law's subjects;

(g) *expression*: the manner in which the law is published, and the various ways in which the wishes of the sovereign are made known;

(h) *remedial appendages*: any such other laws as may be created and published in order to clarify the requirements of the principal law.

JOHN AUSTIN (1790–1859)

ANALYTICAL POSITIVISM AND THE COMMAND THEORY OF LAW

John Austin is generally regarded as being Jeremy Bentham's disciple, being, like the older man, both a positivist and a utilitarian. Austin was ultimately responsible for the popularisation of the command theory of law. He argued for a distinction to be made between 'analytical or expositional jurisprudence', looking at the basic facts of the law, its origin, existence and underlying concepts, and 'normative or censorial jurisprudence', which involved the question of the goodness or badness of the existing law. Austin, like Bentham, argued that the factual questions relating to the existence of the law should be answered before questions of what the law ought to be could be considered. He believed that the more important question for the study of jurists was the question of the factual existence of law, and this he regarded as being the basic subject of jurisprudence.

For Austin, as for Bentham, the existence of law had to do with the same issues of sovereignty, power and sanctions. People with power in a politically independent society would set down rules governing certain acts for those who were in the habit of obeying them. Austin's notion of sovereignty was similar to Jeremy Bentham's.

Austin's definition of law proceeded from the general to the particular, starting with a general characterisation of law as 'a rule laid down for the guidance of an intelligent being by an intelligent being having power over him'. Within this general conception, Austin identified two major divisions:

■ *the laws of God*: laws set by God for his human creatures, which Austin regarded as being 'laws properly so called';

■ *laws set by men to men:* these comprise two distinct categories:

● positive law: laws set by men as political superiors or in the exercise of rights conferred by such superiors;
● positive morality: laws set by men, but not as political superiors or in the exercise or rights conferred by such superiors – these include what Austin calls 'laws by analogy' – for example, rules referring to the membership of private clubs.

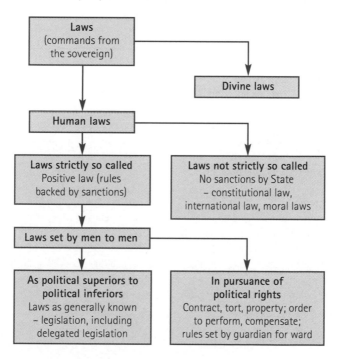

From this, Austin proceeded to make further distinctions which effectively narrowed down his conception of the positive law which he believed should be the proper subject of jurisprudence.

Ultimately, Austin's conception of law can be reduced to the simple statement:

Law is the command of a sovereign backed by sanctions.

THREE ELEMENTS OF AUSTIN'S DEFINITION OF LAW

The three main elements of that conception were explained by Austin as follows:

- Sovereign

  - habitually followed
  - politically superior
  - factually determinable
  - illegally limitable

- Command

  - expression of desire
  - general order
  - threat of sanctions

- Sanction

  - harm, pain or evil
  - minimal possibility
  - possibility of application

Sovereign

The sovereign is the essential source of all law in society and where there is no sovereign there can be no law. The sovereign must be a determinate and common political superior, that is, it must be possible clearly to identify and determine a person (or group of persons) who is habitually obeyed by the bulk of the members of society and who does not habitually obey anybody else. The sovereign must be legally illimitable and indivisible and be the sole source of legal authority.

Command

The sovereign's will is expressed in the form of a command. A command is an imperative form of a statement of the sovereign's wishes, and it is different from an order in that it is general in its application. It is also different from other expressions of will in that it carries with it the threat of a sanction which may be imposed in the event of the subject of the command not complying with it.

Sanction

A sanction is some harm, pain or evil which is attached to a command issued by a sovereign and which is intended as a motivation for the subjects of the sovereign to comply with his or her commands. The sanction is a necessary element of a command and there must be a realistic possibility that it will be imposed in the event of a breach. It is sufficient that there be the threat of the possibility of a minimum harm, pain or evil.

CRITICISMS OF AUSTIN'S COMMAND THEORY

Many of the criticisms of John Austin's command theory of law have concentrated on its inadequacy in explaining the incidence of law and the salient features of present day legal systems. Some of these criticisms, as articulated by Herbert Hart in *The Concept of Law* (1961), can be summarised briefly as follows.

The problem of the continuity of legislative authority

Austin's characterisation of a sovereign requires that the sovereign be identifiable as a matter of fact as the person who is habitually obeyed by the bulk of the members of a society. Such a characterisation poses the problem of the continuity of legislative authority: where a ruling sovereign passes away and a new one is installed, there cannot be in the first instance a habit of obedience to that new sovereign which may give him the authority to make laws. Does this then mean that the new sovereign is no sovereign at all and therefore cannot make valid laws? If this is the case then how can a new habit of obedience be established where the new sovereign's wishes do not have the authority of law, since only a sovereign can be the source of commands which have the pedigree to be laws? It would appear that the new incumbent can never become sovereign in Austin's terms and so can never have the authority to make law. Hart argues that the problem with Austin's model of sovereignty is that he lacks the concept of a legal rule which would simply denote who can or cannot make law in a particular society.

The problem of the persistence of laws

Austin's model characterises all laws as the commands of a sovereign. All laws therefore owe their existence, validity and authority to a particular and determinate sovereign, and practically there can be no law without a sovereign expressing wishes in the form of commands. The problem that this raises is one of the continuing validity of laws when the sovereign who is their author is no longer in existence. How can certain laws continue to exist validly and to be applied authoritatively when those who created them have long passed into oblivion? Austin's answer to this problem was that such laws retain their validity through the 'tacit consent' of the new sovereign. However, the problem with the notion of tacit consent is that it requires that the new sovereign should positively apply his or her mind to the existence of these laws and then consciously make a decision authorising their continuing validity, even if this decision is not expressly communicated or published. The fact of the matter is that in most cases new legislators do not go through this deliberate process of validation of laws preexisting their own assumption of legislative authority. They simply accept the validity of such laws because there normally is a 'rule' in most mature legal systems validating these laws. Austin's problem, again, is that his command theory lacked the notion of such a rule.

The problem of the variety of laws

For Austin, every law must have a sanction for it to have validity, since the imperative conception of law contends that all laws are in the form of commands expressing the will of a sovereign, and a command is distinguished from other expressions of will by the fact that commands invariably carry with them the threat of some harm, pain or evil which may realistically be applied in the event of non-compliance by the subject. One problem which this notion raises is that not all laws carry with them the threat of a sanction. Some laws are merely regulatory, and prescribe how people must act without necessarily threatening punishment. Other laws confer power on people to validly create legal relationships, for example, the laws of contract. An attempt by Austin to treat the nullity of a contract as a sanction for non-compliance with proper contractual procedure appears far fetched, since not all the parties to a contract will suffer from such nullity. Even in the case of laws which carry sanctions, for example, criminal law, sanctions are only appealed to in the event of a breach, and are not necessarily in the forefront of the consideration of either the legislators or their subjects at every stage of the creation and existence of the laws to which they attach.

Other criticisms of Austin's doctrine

Other criticisms of Austin's doctrine include the following:

- The requirement that the sovereign be legally illimitable, which leads Austin to conclude that constitutional law is not law properly so called, fails to explain the fact that the rules comprising most constitutions are regarded by those subject to them as binding law and are deferred to as such. In any case, it is not necessary for legislators themselves to be above the law in order for their legislative activity to produce valid legal instruments.

- Austin's conclusion that international law is not law but 'positive morality merely' because no specific sovereign can be identified as being the author of its rules, and since obedience to these is a matter of choice for the various states, results from a confusion between the lack of the systematic structures normally identified with municipal legal systems and questions of validity of laws. Laws may validly exist even in situations where some of these structures are non-existent or merely embryonic in their development.

- The requirement that the sovereign in a politically independent society be indivisible fails adequately to explain the existence of multiple law-making bodies in some jurisdictions, for example, federalist societies such as the US, as well as in parliamentary democracies where the law-making structures are decentralised. Austin's attempt to equate the entire electorate in such systems with the sovereign would lead to the untenable situation where the electorate would be seen as being in the process of issuing commands to themselves and being in the habit of obeying themselves.

HANS KELSEN (1881–1973)

THE PURE THEORY OF LAW

The rationale and methodology of the pure theory

Hans Kelsen sought to define and identify the essence of law by providing a formula which excluded any factors which might obscure our perception of such law. As a positivist, Kelsen believed that the existence, validity and authority of law had nothing at all to do with such non-legal factors as politics, morality, religion, ethics and so on. He therefore sought to provide a 'pure theory' of law, one that would be scientific and accurate in answering the question: what is the law? In this context, 'pure' means two things: that the analysis of the law is limited to the law itself, and that the analysis of the law is purely conceptual (rather than contextual).

The nature of law as a system of norms

Kelsen regards the law as a coercive system, concerned primarily with the application of sanctions to persons who have acted in certain specific ways. The law is constituted by norms (statements of what ought to be) which inform officials of a State as to the instances when they may apply sanctions to persons whose actions have fulfilled the conditions under which such sanctions must be applied.

These norms express the reality of the law to the people who are tasked with enforcing it, even though the actual rules of the system may be phrased differently.

The distinction between moral norms, legal norms and legal rules

Kelsen distinguishes between a moral norm, which is a required standard of behaviour in relation to some individual or social conception of the good, and a legal norm, which merely describes what the law specifies ought to be under certain circumstances. The legal norm does not in itself prescribe action, it merely describes what the law essentially requires, even though the law itself may not be in the form of an 'ought' proposition. A further distinction is therefore to be made between legal rules, that is, the surface features of law, and legal norms, that is, the internal essence of law. The content of legal norms is, for Kelsen, the essence of all law and is what all legal science should strive to explicate in respect to different societies.

Pure theory of law

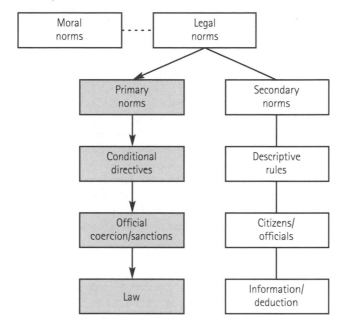

Primary norms and secondary norms

Another way in which Kelsen describes the distinction between legal rules and legal norms is in terms of primary and secondary norms. The primary norm may be seen as that statement which stipulates the sanctions which may be applied under certain conditions. It is the primary norm which constitutes a conditional directive to officials to apply sanctions in certain circumstances. The legal rule, that is, the actual rule created by the law-making authority, and which specifies the proscription or prescription of certain conduct is then only a secondary norm and is not itself the essence of the law. The secondary norm can be derived from the primary norm by a process of deduction.

The subjective and objective meanings of actions

For Kelsen, all actions have a subjective meaning and an objective meaning. An act may have no more significance than that which can be derived from its mere occurrence, for example, the act of picking up a stone and throwing it at a wall may mean only that – the simple physical act of employing one's musculature in the physical elevation of a solid piece of matter and forcefully propelling it in a certain direction with the intention that it collide with another, larger piece of solid matter. This is the subjective meaning of the act, and if there were no law against this sort of activity, then no more would be thought of it and the matter would lie where it fell. However, if there were a law against throwing stones at certain buildings, say, people's homes, then there would be a primary norm which directs officials to apply sanctions in the event of some person acting in a way which fulfils the conditions under which sanctions may be applied under that law. In this case, the act of picking up a stone and throwing it at a wall would automatically acquire legal significance, in that if the wall forms part of some person's abode, then the stone thrower's act will have fulfilled the conditions under which an official would properly be required to apply a sanction by the relevant legal norm. This then becomes the objective meaning of the act. And, in a legal system which is on the whole efficacious, the appropriate sanction would be duly applied.

The hierarchy of norms

Kelsen's legal norms are arranged in a dynamic hierarchy, with each norm deriving its validity from another norm which occupies a position higher up in the hierarchy. These norms range from the general, which are higher norms, to the particular, which are lower norms. The ultimate validity of all legal norms is predicated upon an hypothetical basic norm or *Grundnorm* which occupies the highest position in the hierarchy, and beyond which no other norm may exist. The basic norm can sometimes be identified with, although it is not, the historical first constitution of a society.

The basic norm and the validity of norms

The basic norm is presupposed because the mere contention that a certain norm exists presupposes its validity, and that validity can only be derived from a higher norm, which in turn acquires its validity from an even higher norm, culminating in a valid *Grundnorm*. Thus, the question regarding legal norms, including the basic norm, is not whether or not they are valid, since the mere fact of their existence presupposes their validity, rather it is one of whether or not, in their existence, they belong to a particular hierarchy and hence to a certain legal order.

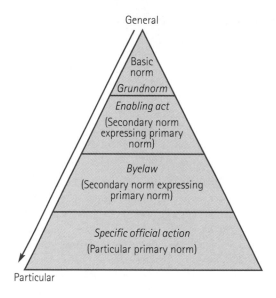

The basic norm and legal efficacy

Every society has a basic norm peculiar to it, and this *Grundnorm* can be identified by reference to the legal norms which are actually referred to by officials in each society when they apply sanctions. It follows that it is only in a society where officials regularly and effectively apply sanctions in accordance with certain primary norms that we can identify a system of norms and hence a basic norm. Kelsen's formula for identifying law as a matter of norms, therefore, hinges upon the efficacy of legal systems in the application of sanctions. It follows, then, that there cannot be a hierarchical system of norms in a society where officials do not efficaciously apply sanctions. If we cannot identify such a system, nor its basic norm, then we cannot be able to identify law in that society. For Kelsen, then, we can properly declare that such a society does not have law nor a legal system. The basic norm is presupposed on account of the actual activity of officials applying sanctions in accordance with primary norms which constitute a system which is on the whole efficacious. It follows that the basic norm can change in situations where officials cease to apply sanctions in accordance with one set of norms and start applying sanctions efficaciously in accordance with another set of norms.

Implications and criticisms of Kelsen's pure theory

Kelsen's theory has been criticised for its extreme emphasis on the formal identification of the elements of law, excluding, as it does, such factors as politics,
morality and questions of justice. Indeed he has been accused of engaging in
'an exercise in logic, not in life', and his theory has been seen as useless as a
device for understanding the complexities of laws and legal systems. It is to be
said, however, that Kelsen's doctrine has a certain value in that it helps us focus
on the actual dynamics of law enforcement, and the fact that ultimately it is
officials who decide how and to what extent the law may affect ordinary
people's lives.

Kelsen's approach, and his emphasis on the role of officials in the occurrence
and existence of the law, meant that he ultimately saw little distinction between
the State and its law. Indeed, Kelsen saw the State as the personification of all
law, and his view thus disregards, to quite a large extent, the perspective of the
ordinary citizens in a society and their interest in the development of the law. In
fact, for Kelsen, it would appear that the common citizenry have no more to do
with the law than merely acting in ways which justify the application of sanctions by officials, and in doing so, their role is merely the passive one of fulfilling
conditions under which sanctions may be applied. Ultimately for Kelsen, only
officials can disobey the law, when they fail to apply a required sanction. This
view appears to be very one sided, emphasising as it does the external, coercive
element of the law, and disregarding the reality that laws are in fact directed at
both officials and ordinary citizens, and that many private persons are keenly
aware of what the law requires of them in certain circumstances and, in most
cases, strive to act in accordance with those requirements out of a sense of
duty, or obligation. For most people, therefore, their activity has both a subjective and an objective meaning.

Kelsen's theory equates the existence of the law with its validity, since legal
norms can exist only in a system which is on the whole efficacious, and such a
system is comprised of a hierarchy of valid legal norms predicated upon a valid
basic norm. Efficacy in this case means merely the regular and effective application of sanctions by 'officials'. What this means is that the validity of laws in
Kelsen's scheme has nothing to do with the legitimacy of the law-making
authority, and indeed, any usurper can create valid laws once they establish
themselves and start to apply sanctions efficaciously, causing the basic norm to
change. In this regard, Kelsen's theory has been criticised for providing

legitimacy to political regimes which do not have a mandate from the citizens to rule and to make law. Certainly, this theory was utilised to try and justify the unilateral assumption of power by an illegal regime in the former Rhodesia in 1965, and to establish the validity of the laws which it subsequently created, in the case of *Madzimbamuto v Lardner-Burke* [1968]. Further, Kelsen's theory does not allow for the criticism of any such valid laws, however iniquitous.

Finally, it must be noted that the identification of the basic norm in any society is an extremely problematic exercise. Since that norm does not have a specific content, and since it is primarily presupposed, its role in the validation of the other norms in the hierarchy can be fraught with obscurities. Since the *Grundnorm* plays such a pivotal role in the validation of the other norms of a system, it follows that any problems which might arise with its identification and explication may affect the entire coherence and consistency of the hierarchy which it supports, and thus deprive the concept of a legal system of its very foundations.

GENERAL CRITICISMS OF THE IMPERATIVE THEORIES

General criticisms of the imperative positivist approaches to law include the following:

- Contrary to the imperative positivist view, legal systems and law do not just rest on sovereignty, power and force. They are based more on legitimacy, authority and obligation.

- For imperative positivists, sanctions are a necessary part of all valid law. However, the fact is that there are many laws which do not have sanctions attached to them. Many laws confer powers on people, or regulate people's conduct in a relatively neutral fashion without threatening punishment.

- Whereas it is true in some cases that, as the imperative positivists argue, people obey laws out of fear of sanctions, this is not the sole motivation in all cases. Sometimes people comply with laws because they feel a sense of obligation arising from their recognition of the legitimacy of the law-making authorities.

- Imperative positivists place a strict distinction between law and morality. In reality, however, many people perceive a link between law and morality.

Especially where questions of justice arise, the stability of the entire legal system and the validity of its laws may depend on the extent to which the majority view a society's laws as conforming to some moral standard.

■ Ultimately, the imperative positivists are criticised for providing an arid and excessively formalistic approach to law. It is argued that there is no value in a theory which cannot explain all the salient features of extant legal systems and/or offer room for improvement. Further, an approach to law which simply legitimises existing structures and institutions even if these are a corruption of law is ultimately inadequate.

You should now be confident that you would be able to tick all the boxes on the checklist at the beginning of this chapter. To check your knowledge of Positivist theories of law why not visit the companion website and take the Multiple Choice Question test. Check your understanding of the terms and vocabulary used in this chapter with the flashcard glossary.

Alternatives to the
imperative models of law

The key alternatives to command models of law are those set out by Hart, Fuller and Dworkin, though it is Hart's work which is the most innovative: it has been said to provide the foundations of contemporary legal philosophy in the English-speaking world and beyond. Hart's work was a reaction against Austin's jurisprudence, which he once referred to as 'the record of a failure' (1961).

Early alternatives to imperative models also include legal realism.

Legal Realism
This movement rejects the notion of natural law because it does not believe in immutable principles of justice, but it also rejects imperative models of the law because for them the meaning of legal terms does not come from the legislator but from an observation of law in action. Legal realism is an empirical reaction to legal formalism, to the idea of a science of law. There are two main movements: American and Scandinavian Legal Realism. The American Critical Legal Studies movement, which emerged in the 1970s, can be said to have arisen out of American Realism (see Chapter 9).

American Realism
American realists see law as an instrument of government designed to achieve, and justify, specific social aims. For them, the meaning of legal terminology, legal values, is acquired through experience and observation as they are 'real'. This movement is often said to have first emerged in the US with Supreme Court Justice Oliver Wendell Holmes. It was prevalent essentially between the 1920s and the 1940s.

Legal realists believe that:

- Legal rules do not determine the outcome of legal disputes, judges do.

- The law is a tool to achieve social goals and balance conflicting interests.

- The study of law should be interdisciplinary because legal outcomes depend on factors which are extrinsic to legal rules.

This movement is characterised by two core premises:

- The study of law involves more than rules and doctrine; it includes the study of how law works in practice, or 'law in action'.

■ Law is an instrument of government. It is a means to achieve social goals, these are not abstract and immutable, but concrete and contingent upon their context.

These premises produce two types of scepticism:

Rule scepticism
For realists, judges do not reach their decisions on the basis of a formalist application of legal rules and principles to the facts of a given case, but reach a decision based on the desirability of a given outcome and only subsequently resort to the rules in order to rationalise their decision in terms that seem to be legally grounded.

Fact scepticism
In the same way that judges use legal rules essentially in order to ground their decision in law rather than applying rules to cases, they also interpret the facts of cases under their consideration in such a way as to fit the outcome that they wish to reach. Events are thus construed in such a way as to warrant the application of the legal rules which will rhetorically ground the judicial argumentation.

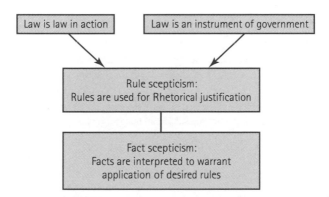

Law should therefore be considered as a policy science. A lasting effect of realism on American legal reasoning is that the legitimacy of a judicial decision stems from both its conformity to rules and precedents but also its social implications.

Scandinavian Legal Realism

The founding father of this movement is the Swede Axel Hägerström (1868–1939). Scandinavian realism is more philosophically grounded than American realism. Its starting point is that what cannot be known through experience does not exist and so should not be taken into consideration in the production of legal knowledge. It follows that natural law does not exist, but also that rights and duties do not exist either. In Hart's words, both schools of realism agree that a right is not an objective entity, 'existing apart from the behaviour of men', but whereas for American realists a right 'is a term by which we describe the prophecies we make of the probable behaviour of courts or officials; the Scandinavian jurists [...] say that a right is nothing real at all but an ideal or fictitious or imaginary power'. This is because the concepts of rights and duties have no empirical content; they do not belong to sensible, material reality: 'these concepts are metaphysical sham-concepts: it is impossible to identify that which we call a right or a duty with any fact' (Olivecrona).

So for Hägerström:

- There are no such things as natural law or natural rights because sensible reality is devoid of values (i.e. it is absurd to ask 'what *ought* to happen in nature', all one can do is ask 'what *does* happen in nature').

- Imperative models of law are invalid because it does not make sense to hold that the meaning of legal terminology is determined by the will of the legislator.

- Laws are found in the reality of social facts.

- Positive law is a system of rules that can be identified empirically as behavioural regularities in human societies.

- Legal knowledge is an empirical inquiry into the causal relations between legal rules and human behaviour.

In this perspective, known as 'rational naturalism', the normativity of law is not accepted. This is why, as soon as the late 1930s, many people saw realism as potentially dangerous because it did away with the necessity to ground legal systems in morality. Fuller's work goes against this perceived error.

HERBERT HART, *THE CONCEPT OF LAW* (1961)

THE THEORETICAL BACKGROUND TO HART'S CONCEPT OF LAW

Hart's background is the analytical school in English philosophy. He presents his approach to law as a superior alternative to previous attempts at explaining the nature of law – especially the imperative positivism of Bentham, Austin and Kelsen – which he believes have provided us only with narrow, singular, and therefore inadequate definitions of the law. Hart argues that it is not possible to answer effectively the question: *what is law?* by appealing to a definition which merely emphasises some particular feature of the law, such as its coercive element or its moral dimension. Such an approach will only serve to obscure other, equally important elements of the law which we cannot afford to ignore if we are to present an adequate picture and explanation of the nature of law.

Hart asserts that the main reason why the question: *what is law?* has not been successfully answered over the years has been because of the continued recurrence of three main issues relating to the nature of law which he believes have never been properly dealt with and explained by previous thinkers on the subject.

THREE RECURRING ISSUES IN JURISPRUDENCE

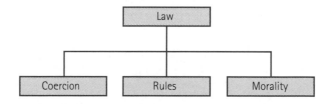

- The question of the relationship between law and coercion: 'How does law differ from, and how is it related to, orders backed by threats?'

- The question of the relationship between law and morality: 'How does legal obligation differ from, and how is it related to, moral obligation?'

- The nature of rules: 'What are rules and to what extent is law an affair of rules?'

For Hart, the efforts to provide a clear-cut definition in answer to the question: *what is law?* have ended with many previous writers on the subject limiting their consideration to only one or other of the above issues. For example, he attempts to show that the imperative theories of law have entirely lacked the concept of a rule, and that this has caused them to regard law only as an external system of coercion, thus ignoring the internal element of legal obligation which leads people to obey laws even when there is no threat of force compelling them to comply.

A related problem is that which arises from what Hart calls the 'open texture' of words and therefore of the law. Law is basically a matter of language – an attempt to communicate required standards of behaviour by the use of words which are supposed to signify some notion of reality. However, words by their very nature are problematic as instruments for such communication, since their meanings may be obscure or their implications may differ depending on the context of the intended recipient of the message. In this regard, definitions may be required of the words used initially, and it is the crux of the problem that any such definitions have themselves to be constructed out of other words, which latter may also be obscure and so require further clarification. According to Hart, this problem has led some thinkers, such as the legal realists, mistakenly to deny that law is a matter of rules and to assert instead that only what the courts say is what constitutes law. For the same reason, Formalists have argued for an approach to rules of law which seeks to limit the choices which might be available in instances when such rules have to be interpreted.

Linked to the above is a problem which results from the fact that the creators of any laws in society are, in Hart's words, 'men not gods'. This means that they have certain limitations which include:

■ *Relative ignorance of fact*: it is never possible, when creating a law to deal with a particular situation, to be absolutely certain that one has included and covered all material issues and the various possible combinations of such issues which may confront anyone seeking to use the law to resolve problems and disputes at a subsequent stage.

■ *Relative indeterminacy of aim*: it is not possible for a legislator accurately to anticipate future developments in society and, therefore, it is difficult to be able to ascertain the best way to deal with new situations which may arise and to which existing laws may need to be applied.

A further problem which Hart identifies is the existence of areas of uncertainty as to what constitutes law and what does not. In this regard, international law and so called 'customary law' are cases in point, as both appear to lack some of the features which are normally associated with law, such as a legislature or a system of courts. Simplistic and singular definitions of law would then tend to exclude these categories of legal phenomena without providing an explanation as to why they should not be treated as law.

THE NEED FOR A FRESH START

Hart believes that generally the above-mentioned problems are a result of the fact that law is a complex social phenomenon which is linked to other social phenomena in various ways.

This makes it difficult to answer the question: *what is law?* effectively through sweeping singular definitions. He notes several previous and contemporary attempts and then concentrates on the command theory of law in order to demonstrate the problems that these have created.

This approach misses one very important point. This is the fact that the laws of many societies are generally obeyed by their citizens, not through the fear of sanctions, but because of a certain sense of obligation arising from the citizen's respect for the legitimacy and authority of the law giver. This is the case even where the individual may not agree with the requirements of a particular law.

Hart argues that the command theorists, in emphasising force as the core component of all law, have looked only on one side of the coin – the external element of law which compels people to act out of fear. This may be the 'bad man's view' of the law and Hart argues that it does not present a balanced picture. In focusing only on the commands of a sovereign and the actions of officials in imposing sanctions, the command theorists have ignored the internal element which characterises all law. This is what Hart calls the 'internal point of view' which makes people feel a sense of obligation to obey the law. Hart makes a distinction between the two notions (see figure overleaf).

THE TWO ASPECTS OF LAW

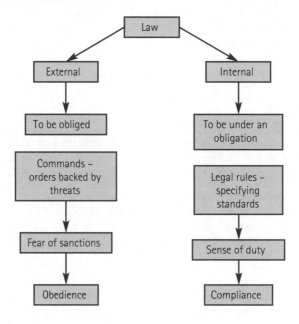

- ■ 'To be obliged' – that is, to be forced to act in a certain way because of some threat, such as when an armed man orders a person to hand over money.

- ■ 'To be under an obligation' – that is, to feel within oneself a sense of duty to act in a certain way without some external stimulus compelling such action.

He argues that the command theories explain law only in terms of the former notion, and that to this extent they are inadequate, because the law operates both in an external and an internal fashion to induce compliance. Indeed, Hart contends that the law functions less as an external and more as an internal inducement to action and that the external element comes into play only in the occasional event of a breach, when officials act to apply sanctions.

Hart believes that the main problem with the command theories of law is that they lack the concept of a rule, which he describes as a statement of an 'accepted standard of behaviour'. Where there is a rule – in this case, a rule of law – which most people are aware of, then there is no need to have officials constantly watching over citizens to see that they comply with the law, because most of these citizens would comply anyway since they accept the rule as standard. They use the rule to judge their own as well as other people's behaviour. They use the standard as a basis for criticism of any behaviour, their own and others', which does not comply with the rule, and they use the rule as a justification for such criticism.

RULES AND THE EXTERNAL/INTERNAL ELEMENTS OF LAW

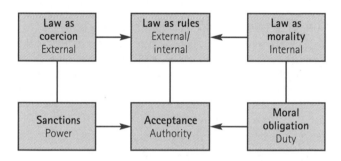

Some of the more specific criticisms which Hart makes of the command theories of law have been noted in the previous chapter. The conclusion which Hart reaches through his examination of the flaws in the imperative approach is that he has effectively established the need for a fresh start. This, he argues, must be a theory of law which avoids singular definitions of the subject. He therefore presents *The Concept of Law* (1961) as an attempt to provide an understanding of law, coercion and morality as interrelated but distinct social phenomena. In this regard, his approach is an 'exercise in analytical jurisprudence', for it is intended to analyse especially the nature of rules in order to determine how legal rules make the law a distinctive form of social control. However, Hart recognises that the law is a social phenomenon which can only be adequately understood and explained in terms of social facts. These facts include the attitudes which people have and the language which they use in expressing their conceptions of the law as well as other social phenomena, such as morality and coercion. For Hart, therefore, his approach must also be seen as an 'exercise in descriptive sociology', for it seeks to explain the law in terms of its social context.

Hart is, however, a committed positivist and his intention is to provide an improved positivist account of the law. He believes that only that which has been created and posited by the proper law-making authorities in a particular society can properly be called law. There is no necessary link between law and morality, and although there may be similarities between them and in their requirements, the two must still be kept strictly separate. Laws are valid if they have been created in accordance with the requirements of proper law making in a certain society, and their goodness or badness has no bearing on their validity.

THE UNION OF PRIMARY AND SECONDARY RULES

For Hart, law is a matter of rules. Rules are statements of accepted standards of behaviour. Law is a system of social rules and to this extent it is similar to morality, which is also constituted of social rules. Both types of rules are 'social' because they arise within a social context, apply to social activity, and have social consequences. However, the rules of law are different from those of morality in a number of fundamental ways.

THE UNION OF PRIMARY AND SECONDARY RULES

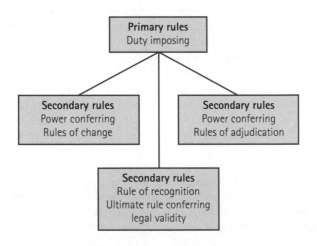

THE SYSTEMATIC QUALITY OF LEGAL RULES

The main distinctive element of law is that its rules have what Hart calls 'a systematic quality'. What this means is that rules of law are of different types, and that each of these categories interacts with the others in a manner which enables them to be called a system rather than say, a 'body', of rules. Rules of morality generally lack this systemic quality. The rules of law can be classified into two main groups, and it is the interaction between these groups which justifies the description of legal arrangements in certain societies as being a legal system.

CATEGORIES OF LEGAL RULES

Primary rules

These are the basic duty-imposing rules of law. They specify what people ought and ought not to do, and in this way they create obligations with which members of a society are required to comply. Examples are rules of the criminal law, tort and so on. In the more mature legal systems, these rules are normally created, validated, enforced and changed by officials.

However, it is possible to envisage a 'pre-legal' society, that is, a society where there may not exist structures such as a legislature, courts and so on. In such a society, there may still be rules of law, because there would be certain rules which are accepted by the majority of the citizens as specifying accepted standards of behaviour, and to which weight and authority are given by consensus. The validity of these rules as law would then depend on what Hart calls the 'internal point of view' of the citizens in the community, which describes a critical reflective attitude enabling the citizens to feel a sense of obligation to obey such laws. This type of arrangement would not, however, be a legal system as such and it would raise a number of problems for the citizens.

- The problem of uncertainty – it would always be difficult to determine whether a certain rule was a rule of law or whether it was some other type of rule, such as a rule of morality, custom or religion.

- The problem of the static nature of laws – even where rules of law were known, new situations might arise which would need the immediate modification of an existing rule to cover that situation or, failing that, the creation of an entirely new rule to resolve a problem. It would not be easy to create, with sufficient expedition, a new rule through the process of establishing consensus amongst all the citizens.

■ The problem of inefficiency – where rules of law were broken, there would always be a difficulty in ascertaining the reality and extent of the breach, as well as in determining the extent of compensation or the severity of punishment. Self-help schemes in this respect would result in a wastage of resources.

In order to resolve these difficulties, there would be a need for a different set of rules, which would determine the processes of creation, validation, transformation and adjudication in respect of the primary rules of law.

Secondary rules

These are rules about rules, that is, they are rules of law which are brought into existence for the purpose of governing the creation and operation of the primary rules and in order to resolve the problems which have been identified above in regard to a legal arrangement in which only primary rules exist. Generally, secondary rules are power-conferring rules, in the sense that they give the ability to some person or body of persons to do something with regard especially to primary rules, although such power may be exercised in respect to other secondary rules as well. A criterion for the existence of a legal system is the acceptance of secondary rules by officials as well as of primary rules by a majority of subjects.

Secondary rules are of three types, corresponding to the problems which may arise in a pre-legal society.

1 *The rule of recognition.* This is the ultimate rule which determines the existence and validity of all other rules in a legal system. Although it is classified as a secondary rule, it lies at the heart of a legal system because it is by reference to it that any other rule can be classified as a rule of law. The rule of recognition therefore resolves the problem of uncertainty as to the legality and validity of rules. It is itself identified by determining the formal criteria by which officials in a particular legal system decide what rules are valid rules of law. So, the rule of recognition may not be written down or even clearly set out as a singular rule. Indeed it may be a conglomeration of rules setting out the accepted formal sources of law in a society. Thus, for example, in England and Wales the main part of the rule of recognition may be in the form:

Whatever the Queen-in-Parliament enacts is law.

This would mean that the legality and validity of most rules in this legal system would depend on whether they have been properly enacted by the Queen-in-Parliament. However, since there are other, accepted, formal sources of law in this country, this would mean that various other elements would have to be added on to the main part of the rule. Thus we could have a more comprehensive rule of recognition which would include these others as sources of valid law, and the full version of the rule of recognition would be, if properly set out, something as follows:

Whatever the Queen-in-Parliament enacts, and whatever byelaws and regulations are enacted in pursuance of the requirements of and in accordance with the powers set out in the enabling statutes, and whatever rules originating from custom are properly judged to be law by the courts, and whatever precedents are at present accepted by the higher courts of the land as accurately specifying the proper interpretation and application of the laws of this country, shall be the valid laws of England and Wales.

The rule of recognition resolves the problems of uncertainty in the law by establishing a formal distinction between those rules which are law and those which are not. In doing so it provides certain rules, both primary and secondary, with both legality and validity. Thus, the rule of recognition will help to determine the separation between legal rules and other social rules such as those of morality, and other factors determining how people should act, such as certain forms of coercion.

2 *The rules of change.* Rules of change are necessary to enable changes to be made in the legal obligations which people may have under the duty-imposing primary rules of a legal system. Such changes may be in the public sphere, where the State imposes certain duties on citizens, or they may be in the private sphere, where citizens create certain legally binding obligations amongst themselves. Thus, rules of change will be of two types:

(i) *Private rules of change*: these enable changes to be made in the legal relationships which private persons have with one another, for example, the rules of contract law. Such rules confer power, rather than impose duties on citizens in their private capacity.

(ii) *Public rules of change*: these rules give power to officials in their public legislative capacity to change the primary and other rules of a legal system in order to meet new developments in the legal needs of society.

Rules of change, then, exist in a legal system to resolve the problem which may arise in a 'pre-legal' situation in respect to the various laws being static and not being capable of expeditious change to cover new and unprecedented situations.

3 *The rules of adjudication.* These rules confer power on judicial officials to carry out the process of adjudication where a dispute has arisen or a law has been breached. They also set out standards for the proper determination by the courts of the instances, the extent and the commensurate punishment or compensation for any breach of the law. These rules exist to resolve the problems of inefficiency which might arise in a 'pre-legal' society where there would be no courts to adjudicate and no way of knowing for certain when a rule of law has been broken and how the situation should be dealt with.

In the 'union of primary and secondary rules', Hart believes that he has found 'not only the heart of a legal system, but a most powerful tool for the analysis of much that has puzzled both the jurist and the political theorist'. He believes that this approach is superior to previous attempts to explain the nature of law. This is because it allows us to see legal phenomena, not in terms of isolated precepts with no meaningful link to social reality, not in the form of disparate chunks of legislative or other obstacles to certain activity, but as a unified system of social control which is predicated upon the concept of the rule of recognition. This, then, requires and enables us to explain the related notions of 'legislation, jurisdiction, validity and, generally, of legal powers, private and public'.

LON FULLER AND THE 'INNER MORALITY OF LAW'

Fuller wrote *The Morality of Law* in 1964, discussing the connection between law and morality. His challenge to the positivist approach to law rejects Hart's conception of the law essentially as a matter of rules with no necessary moral content. The two jurists' disagreement on the nature of law led to the Hart–Fuller Debate in 1958, which was very significant in framing the modern conflict between positivism and natural law.

MORALITY OF LAW

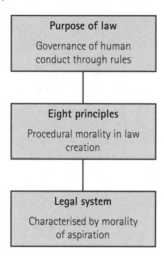

Purpose of law

Governance of human
conduct through rules

Eight principles

Procedural morality in law
creation

Legal system

Characterised by morality
of aspiration

FULLER'S ARGUMENT FOR PROCEDURAL MORALITY IN LEGAL SYSTEMS

The purpose of legal systems

Generally, Fuller takes the opposite stance to the positivist view which argues for a strict separation between law and morals. Fuller saw a necessary connection between law and morality through what he regarded as 'reason' in legal ordering. His main argument is that the basic idea underlying and justifying the creation of a legal system is the purposive enterprise of subjecting human conduct to the governance of rules. In order for a system of social control to be a system of law – as opposed to, say, a system of coercion – it must acknowledge certain procedural purposes, described by a certain set of principles, as its goals.

The morality of legal systems

Fuller argues that legal systems must be set up so that they operate in a manner which will effectively satisfy the ultimate purpose of all legal systems: that is, the governance of human conduct through rules of law. The principles which constitute the basic requirements for a legal system to satisfy this goal constitute what Fuller described as 'the inner morality of law'. These principles are 'internal' because the goals which they describe are themselves intrinsic to the whole idea of law and contribute to its purpose and therefore to the justification for its creation. They are moral because they provide standards for the evaluation of official action in the creation and application of law.

The principles of procedural morality in legislation

Fuller argued for eight principles of proper law making. These were as follows:

1 *There must be rules*: law must be constituted by rules specifying the conduct which is their object and how that conduct is to be controlled. Rules have an ongoing existence after their creation. Law cannot be constituted by *ad hoc* stipulations in the form of capricious orders and commands.

2 *The rules must be prospective and not retrospective*: if human conduct is to be governed by rules, then those whose conduct is to be the object of such governance must be informed in advance of the fact, so that they can plan and organise their activities accordingly. Retrospective laws have the effect of penalising people for actions which were not unlawful at the time when they were perpetrated. The result is to deprive the legal arrangement of any semblance of a system which it could possibly have.

3 *The rules must be published*: as with the above stipulation, people need to know the categories of their conduct which are to be governed by rules of law and the manner in which that governance is to be achieved. Proper publication of the rules of law provides such information and therefore is essential for the operation of law as a system.

4 *The rules must be intelligible*: people cannot be expected to comply with the requirements of the law in the organisation of their activity if they are ignorant of those requirements. Publication of the rules must, therefore, be in a manner which is clear, precise and accurate.

5 *The rules must not be contradictory*: where rules of law contradict each other, the citizen will be confused as to which rule to give precedence to. In this regard, then, it would be improper and indeed self-defeating to require compliance with rules in instances where the citizen does not know whether certain conduct will be deemed unlawful or not.

6 *Compliance with the rules must be possible*: rules requiring the impossible will, of necessity, not be complied with and so it is pointless for us to produce such rules, unless the intention is to penalise citizens unnecessarily.

7 *The rules must not be constantly changing*: certainty is an essential element of the law as a system of rules, for it is only when citizens can predict the consequences of their actions with a fair degree of accuracy, that they can meaningfully plan their actions.

8 *There must be a congruency between the rules as declared and published and the actions of officials responsible for the application and enforcement of such rules*: this enables citizens to be reasonably certain that their actions will attract certain reactions from the system. In this way, citizens can apply the rules of law to themselves with relative confidence and be assured of the results of their actions.

THE LEGALITY OF LEGAL SYSTEMS

Fuller argues that it is only when a system satisfies all the eight principles of proper law making to some degree, that it can be called a legal system. Where there is a complete failure to comply with any of the principles, then whatever the system in question produces is not law but something else, since only a legal system can produce law, and only compliance with all of the eight principles can qualify a system as legal.

The morality of legal systems is a 'morality of aspiration', in that legal systems aspire to comply satisfactorily with the eight principles. It is possible for a system to be more or less of a legal system, depending on the extent to which it satisfies all the eight principles.

Hart takes exception to Fuller for his description of the eight principles as 'moral', arguing that it is possible for a system to comply with all the principles and still succeed in making bad law. Fuller, however, believes that where a system complies with all the principles, then the cumulative effect of such compliance is more likely to be the creation of morally good laws rather than bad ones.

RONALD DWORKIN'S CONCEPTION OF LAW AND MORALITY

Dworkin is best known for his critique of Hart's legal positivism in *Law's Empire*.

DWORKIN'S THEORETICAL STANCE

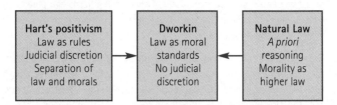

Ronald Dworkin occupies a theoretical position which rejects some of the basic tenets of Natural Law theory and yet which is at the same time extremely critical of the positivist approach to law. It has been said that his ideas constitute a third theory of law, since he appears to occupy a middle ground between positivism and Natural Law without identifying meaningfully with either of them. In fact Dworkin adopts a relativistic view of morality.

Dworkin disagrees with the approach of Natural Law thinking to the question of the nature of law in three respects:

1   He rejects the *a priori* reasoning of Natural Law thinkers which assumes the existence of predetermined moral principles, which, in turn, are supposed to determine the validity of all made laws and to which the latter must approximate.

2   For Dworkin, the close link which Natural Law thinking places between the notion of justice and the fact of law and which makes it impossible to distinguish between the validity of a law and its injustice is implausible.

3   Dworkin also rejects the claim of Natural Law that the truth of propositions of law must be determined on the basis of some moral standard and that the more accurate interpretation of a statute is the one which accords most closely with some moral perspective.

Dworkin disagrees strongly with the three most basic tenets of positivism:

1   The notion that law is made up of only one, factually identifiable and objectively verifiable type of standard. Dworkin specifically singles out the contention advanced by Herbert Hart, that law is composed only of rules.

2   The contention that questions of law and issues of morality must be kept strictly separate when the nature of law is being investigated.

3 The attribution by legal positivists of extensive discretion, amounting almost to legislative power, to judges when they are involved in the adjudication of 'hard cases'.

DWORKIN'S CRITICISM OF HART'S POSITIVISM

The positivist identification of law

Dworkin's main criticism of the positivist approach to law has to do with its general conception of the law as being constituted by only one of a number of different types of standards. The classical positivists, Bentham and Austin, saw law as a set of commands issued by a sovereign who had the power to impose sanctions. Kelsen regarded law as a set of primary norms, that is, conditional directives to officials to apply sanctions under certain circumstances. Hart saw law as a system of primary and secondary rules validated by a rule of recognition. For all these theorists, as positivists, a single type of general standard constituted law, and everything else which did not fit in with the criteria set out for identifying such law was not legally relevant. But Dworkin rejects Hart's conception of the rule of recognition as a master *rule* because it cannot deal with the complex, shifting nature of *principles*. The distinction between *rules* and *principles* is therefore absolutely central to Dworkin's approach.

The differences between rules and principles

Dworkin distinguishes between rules and principles in the following manner. In the process of adjudication, principles apply or operate differently from rules. Where a rule applies, it does so in an 'all or nothing' fashion, requiring that the case be decided or the dispute resolved in accordance with it. Where a principle applies, however, it does not do so in a conclusive fashion. It provides a reason for the case to be decided in a certain way, but does not require that the decision be necessarily in accordance with it. This is because it is possible for principles to conflict, and in such situations they have to be weighed and balanced against each other before the decision is made to apply one or the other.

Because of their propensity to conflict, principles have weight, a quality or dimension which allows them to be compared, balanced, and for choices to be made between them. Rules do not have weight in this sense. The validity or invalidity of rules is not debatable. Either a rule is valid or it is not. Either a rule applies to a particular case or it does not. There is no question of balancing rules one against the other.

Because they do not have the weight of principles, rules cannot conflict and remain both valid. Principles can, however, both be valid and legally binding even if they conflict.

Positivism, hard cases and judicial discretion

Dworkin saw the inability of the positivists to recognise any other standards as being law as a weakness which ultimately led them erroneously to propose that in situations where there was no specific law applying to a particular situation – so called 'hard cases' – then judges were liable to use their discretion in order to reach a decision. In this respect, Dworkin specifically criticised Hart's concept of law as a system of rules.

According to Hart's scheme, only those rules which satisfy the criteria of legal validity set out in a legal system's rule of recognition may be classified as law. Anything else, including rules of morality and other social standards, cannot be law and will therefore not be directly relevant in the processes of adjudication carried out by the courts. Normally, judges will not have any problems identifying the rules of law which apply to a particular dispute and using them to resolve the dispute.

However, in 'hard cases', judges sometimes do run out of law. Such 'hard cases' occur in instances where there is no rule of law which specifically applies to the case before the court. Alternatively, what rules exist may be in irreconcilable conflict with each other and thus cannot be meaningfully utilised. For Hart, as for the other positivists, judges in this situation will use their discretion to decide the matter. This means that they will appeal to their own personal conceptions of what is just and unjust along with, maybe, a consideration of certain matters of policy before they make a decision based on their conception of what is fair. The process of adjudication in these situations then amounts almost to legislation, giving judges the ability either to make new law or fundamentally to alter the meaning and range of application of existing laws. Dworkin argues that this positivist approach does not accurately reflect and explain what in fact happens when courts make decisions in 'hard cases'.

DWORKIN'S 'ONE RIGHT ANSWER' THESIS

Moral standards and the law

Dworkin believes that the law is made up not just of rules, but also of other standards such as policies and principles. These are equal to rules in terms of importance and effect in the processes of legislation and adjudication respectively, although they are different in their character and mode of operation from rules. All these standards together make up what Dworkin calls the 'moral fabric' of a society and are intended to protect certain interests which are regarded by the members of such a society as being valuable. These interests are normally specified in terms of abstract rights, such as the right to life, liberty and human dignity. Each society may have certain abstract rights peculiar to itself, since people in different societies may regard different interests as being valuable and therefore deserving of protection. Thus, a certain 'morality' in this sense may be particular to a certain society, and it will be possible for us to empirically discover that morality by objectively determining what interests are protected by abstract rights in that society. This is what leads Dworkin to reject the Natural Law contention that we can, through reason alone, discover moral principles which are higher than the human will and which are universal, eternal and immutable. The idea of rights, however, still allows him to argue that morality is or should be a part of law, and that considerations of justice do, and must, carry weight in the determination of disputes by the courts.

Hercules and the limits of judicial discretion

Where a case comes before a court of law, the judge is not just limited to applying one set of standards, such as rules, to resolve the dispute. There are available to him other standards, such as principles, to make a decision even in cases where no specific rule of law applies. These principles will constrain the judge to make a certain and specific decision and therefore limit his or her discretion in adjudication.

For Dworkin, judges do not have quasi-legislative discretion. They do not have discretion in the 'strong sense' of being actually able to make decisions which have the effect of producing new law or fundamentally altering existing laws. They may have discretion in the 'weak sense' in the manner in which they apply the law as found in rules and principles. This is because, although judges are not provided with specific procedures for applying each law, they still must not act in a mechanical fashion and must exercise a degree of judgment in the interests of justice and fairness.

Ultimately, because of the existence and operation of legal principles, there is in relation to every dispute always a right answer to the question: *who has a right to win?* All a judge needs to do is to find that answer, and in doing so he or she must search through the 'moral fabric' of society.

To illustrate his argument, Dworkin appeals to actual decided cases where he says the use of legal principles is evident. One such case is the American case of *Riggs v Palmer* [1899], where the question arose as to whether a murderer could be allowed to inherit from his victim, even though the will deposing the estate in his favour was valid. Under the applicable rules of testamentary succession, the murderer was entitled to inherit, since there was no provision for an exception in relation to this particular situation. The court, however, relying on the legal principle which says that no person may profit from his or her wrong, decided to deny the murderer the inheritance. For Dworkin, this principle justifies a decision which at that time could not have properly been made under any existing rule of law. At the same time, however, the application of the principle resulted in a decision which had as much legal authority as if it had been made under a legal rule. This shows that there are always legal standards underpinning judicial decisions in 'hard cases', even where the existence and application of such standards is not always articulated by the respective judges.

To further reinforce his argument, Dworkin postulates a hypothetical judge, appropriately named Hercules, whom he endows with superhuman powers of analysis, deduction and adjudication. Hercules has the capacity to provide exhaustive justifications for decisions in 'hard cases' on the grounds of principle. In order to do this, Hercules would initially have to construct the most sound theory of law possible which will provide moral and political justification for the legal rules and institutions comprising 'law' in his particular jurisdiction.: the theory that *best fits* and justifies the law as a whole (law as integrity) will be the one used to decide a particular case. This theory, if properly worked out, would represent the law as a seamless web of legal rules, legal principles and other legal standards capable of providing a single right answer in every instance where the question arises: *who has a right to win?* Hercules would thus be able to justify every correct decision in respect to 'hard cases' by appealing to the soundest theory and to the standards of adjudication which it specifies.

Unfortunately, no judge possesses Hercules' 'superhuman skill, learning, patience and acumen', and thus judges are not capable of providing these exhaustive justifications for their decisions in 'hard cases' in every instance. However, the point which Dworkin is making by positing the ideal judge is basically, that the process of adjudication in 'hard cases' is not as haphazard and capricious an affair as the positivist reliance on the notion of judicial discretion would imply. Judges do seek to find justification for decisions which they make in such cases, and in many of them, such justification exists, even though it may not be specifically articulated by the judge in question.

Of course, sometimes, judges make mistakes in deciding 'hard cases' and, sometimes, they do not properly apply the correct principles in a manner which would provide them with a right answer. But this is only a result of the fallibility of judges as human beings and does not invalidate the correctness of other decisions made on the same basis. The fact that most judges do not provide proper explanations and justifications for their decisions in 'hard cases' does not mean that those explanations and justifications do not exist.

You should now be confident that you would be able to tick all the boxes on the checklist at the beginning of this chapter. To check your knowledge of Alternatives to the imperative models of law why not visit the companion website and take the Multiple Choice Question test. Check your understanding of the terms and vocabulary used in this chapter with the flashcard glossary.

5

Utilitarianism

JEREMY BENTHAM AND CLASSICAL UTILITARIANISM AS QUANTITATIVE HEDONISM

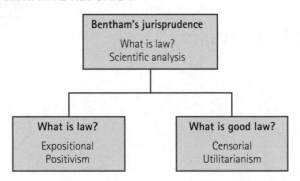

BENTHAM AS BOTH POSITIVIST AND UTILITARIAN

As a legal theorist, Jeremy Bentham was a positivist who regarded an over-whelmingly important field of jurisprudential inquiry to be that of answering the question: *what is law?* in terms of the empirically demonstrable facts of power, sovereignty and sanctions. He was also a renowned reformer, who believed that the process of legislation should be geared towards the realisation of 'the good', which in turn meant that all legislation must be aimed at providing abundance and security, and at the reduction of inequalities between citizens in society. Bentham, however, rejected the approach of Natural Law thinkers which sought to identify the 'good' in law with some higher set of moral principles derivable by reason from some metaphysical source such as nature or God.

Bentham also expressed a profound hostility for the methods of English common law in general, and for judicial law making in particular. As such, he was a strong advocate of codification, which by definition implies the need of going beyond the question of what law is and towards the question of what law should be. Bentham invented a number of devices designed to create good law.

THE PRINCIPLE OF UTILITY

Bentham believed that the most important quality of human beings was their sentience – that is, their ability to feel pleasure (which he regarded as good and therefore to be pursued and maximised) and pain (which was bad and had to be reduced). Bentham argued that these were self-evidently the two masters of humankind. He identified what he called 'pleasures of the sense', such as riches, power, friendship, good reputation and knowledge, among other things. There were also pains of the sense, including privation, enmity, bad reputation, malevolence, fear, etc.

For Bentham, the principle of utility had to be the guiding standard and the basis for evaluation of all action. Utility in this case was to be understood as that quality of an object or action which gave it a propensity to produce some good, satisfaction/happiness or benefit on the one hand, and to prevent or reduce pain, evil or mischief on the other. The principle of utility was, as such, an objective standard for deciding on what was good law and what was not.

THE *FELICIFIC CALCULUS* AND THE MAXIMISATION OF HAPPINESS

Bentham believed that it was possible to predict accurately the consequences of an act and to calculate the extent to which it would promote pleasure and prevent pain. He believed that we could actually measure the intensity, duration, purity and fecundity of these sensations, and he developed a 'felicific/ hedonistic calculus' for achieving this. Taking into account the certainty, propinquity (i.e. how distant the expected benefits are) and the extent of such sensations, we could calculate the social totals of the amount of pleasure and pain which an action would have. By making a quantitative comparison between these, we could then choose to perpetrate only those actions, or enact only those laws, which would have the overall effect of providing for the *greatest happiness of the greatest number*.

For Bentham, the 'science of legislation' comprised the ability, on the part of the law-making authorities in a State, meaningfully to tell or predict the sort of actions and measures which would maximise pleasure or happiness and minimise pain or misery. The 'art of legislation' was then the ability of the legislators to create laws which would effectively promote the good and reduce the bad in this sense.

THE *FELICIFIC CALCULUS*

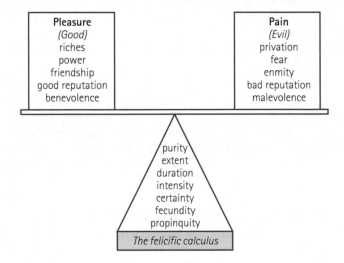

Pleasure	Pain
(Good)	*(Evil)*
riches	privation
power	fear
friendship	enmity
good reputation	bad reputation
benevolence	malevolence

purity
extent
duration
intensity
certainty
fecundity
propinquity

The felicific calculus

THREE BASIC ASSUMPTIONS OF UTILITARIANISM

The logic of Jeremy Bentham's utilitarianism was grounded on three basic assumptions:

1 The happiness of an individual person is augmented in circumstances where the addition made to the sum total of their pleasures is greater than any addition made to the sum total of their pains.

2 The general interest of a community consists of all the interests of the individuals which it comprises.

3 The collective happiness of a community is increased in circumstances where the total of all pleasures of the individual members of that community is augmented to a greater extent than their pains.

UTILITARIANISM AND SOCIAL HAPPINESS

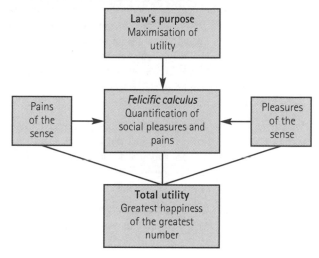

THE PANOPTICON

Lastly, there is a less 'benevolent' aspect to Bentham's quantitative hedonism, which is that it rests on absolute surveillance. For Bentham the principle of utility needs an institutional device to be implemented efficiently. Indeed it is clearly the case that the extension of the *felicific calculus* to all inhabitants of a given territory – this *calculus* being cast as the sole legitimising device for law by Bentham – has to be mediated by the constant surveillance of all by all. Infinitesimal calculation of pain and pleasure requires absolute knowledge and so absolute visibility.

Thus Bentham, with the help of his architect brother, took his utilitarian theory in the practical direction by coming up with the design of an institution which he called the Panopticon. In the Panopticon there would be a central tower in which a watcher would be (or not) situated, keeping everyone in check through the (real or imagined) operation of his gaze. The key practical application of the Panopticon was clearly the prison, but Bentham thought the Panopticon could be used for all manner of purposes:

> No matter how different, or even opposite, the purpose: whether it be that of punishing the incorrigible, guarding the insane, reforming the

vicious, confining the suspected, employing the idle, maintaining the helpless, curing the sick, instructing the willing in any branch of industry, or training the rising race in the path of education: in a word, whether it be applied to the purposes of perpetual prisons in the room of death, or prisons for confinement before trial, or penitentiary-houses, or houses of correction, or work-houses, or manu-factories, or mad-houses, or hospitals, or schools.

(*Panopticon or the Inspection House, etc.*: 1962, vol. IV, 40)

Note: The panoptic mechanism invented by Bentham has been convincingly interpreted by Michel Foucault in his remarkable *Discipline and Punish* (1977) as characteristic of a transition between a form of political power enforced by the sovereign and one that operates through networks of surveillance.

SOME CRITICISMS OF BENTHAM'S UTILITARIANISM (see also Chapter 6)
Some of the more specific criticisms of the Benthamite utilitarian creed have to do with its coherence and the consistency of its requirements. These criticisms include the following:

■ Generally, utilitarian theory is based upon the assumption that it is possible to predict the consequences of a particular action or law, thus enabling prior evaluation to be made of an act in terms of the extent to which it will maximise pleasure and minimise pain. The contrary view is that, in practice, it is not possible to look into the future with such clarity of vision as to be able to determine how a certain arrangement will turn out. The assertion that it is somehow feasible to evaluate the goodness or badness of actions and laws in terms of consequences, prior to the event, is therefore essen-tially fallacious.

■ The idea of the *felicific calculus* by which we are supposed to be able to measure the sum total of pains and pleasures flowing from a contemplated act is impracticable. Pain and pleasure are simply too subjective to be measured accurately, let alone for them to be compared one to the other in quantitative terms. The whole idea of being able to calculate the extent to which the happiness of a community generally has been augmented and the extent to which the sum total of its misery has been reduced is based upon an empirically indefensible proposition. To this extent, the principle of utility, as a standard for evaluating actions and laws, is not altogether objective and is no better than the moral principles proposed by Natural Law thinkers.

■ Utilitarian theory provides what is essentially a consumer model of law, representing a scenario in which the law makers in a society practically go shopping around, picking out those measures which, in their opinions, best satisfy certain perceived desires amongst the members of their community. In the first place, the truth of the matter is that legislators do not pick and choose legislative measures in this way. In creating certain legal arrangements, their actions are determined and influenced by a whole range of other factors such as efficiency and convenience, as well as other values apart from the mere pursuit of happiness. In any case, it is accepted that the desires of people in society are capable of being manipulated in various ways. This means that what the legislators treat as the desires of their subjects may not necessarily be the genuine article, and, therefore, the consequences of any action may not be accurately predictable.

■ Finally, it is argued, the linchpin of Bentham's utilitarianism – the pursuit of happiness and the satisfaction of basic sensual desires – is a rather gross and perverse aim for morality. Utilitarianism is a moral philosophy which seeks to provide a theory of justice. Surely the noble ideal of justice demands a more refined conception of good and bad and a more rigorous standard for evaluating law than this basic pandering to unbridled hedonism?

JOHN STUART MILL AND THE REFINEMENT OF UTILITARIANISM THEORY: UTILITARIANISM AS A QUALITATIVE ALTRUISM

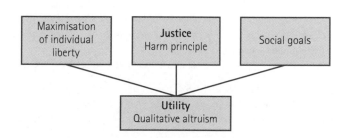

UTILITARIANISM AND THE NATURE OF HAPPINESS: QUALITY V QUANTITY

John Stuart Mill (1806–73) sought to refine the Benthamite version of utilitarian theory by adopting a qualitative approach to the main requirements of that theory.

THE SOURCES OF SATISFACTION/HAPPINESS

Bentham argued for the maximisation of happiness and the minimisation of misery purely in the physical sense, that of sensual pleasure and pain. Mill argued that there were other sources of happiness which were of a different nature, but which provided as much satisfaction and were as valuable as pleasures of the sense.

THE FORMS OF SATISFACTION/HAPPINESS

Bentham believed that it was possible to measure the quantity of happiness and misery using the *felicific calculus*. The difference in quantity is the only real difference between pleasures and pains. The proper test of the 'goodness' or 'badness' of an act is the amount of happiness or misery which it produces. Mill argued that there are qualitative as well as quantitative differences between sources of happiness and misery. A proper test of the goodness or badness of an act needs to make reference to the quality, as well as to the quantity, of the pleasures and pains produced.

THE VALUE OF SATISFACTION/HAPPINESS

For Bentham, the value of pleasures depends merely on the differences in quantity between them. Mill, however, argued that the quality of satisfaction or pleasure produced by an act is as important, if not even more important than the quantity produced. He believed that the differences in quality between pleasures may mean that small amounts of some pleasures are regarded by those experiencing them as being of much greater value than large amounts of other, less refined, pleasures.

THE NATURE OF HUMAN BEINGS

Bentham placed emphasis on the sentience of human beings – that is, their ability to feel pleasure or pain – in working out the requirements of utilitarian theory. This led him to consider only the physical sensations of pain and pleasure, as elements of misery and happiness. Mill believed that intelligence, rather than sentience, was a more important characteristic of human beings. The full use of one's higher faculties, therefore, could lead to a greater, truer and qualitatively more valuable happiness than the mere satisfaction of base physical pleasures.

UTILITARIANISM AND THE NEED FOR HAPPINESS: HEDONISM v ALTRUISM

Mill's consideration of the justification and the process of the utilitarian search for collective social happiness led him to different conclusions from those reached by Bentham:

■ Bentham argued that, in the pursuit of happiness, people are or should be motivated to secure the happiness of others, because by doing so they ensure their own happiness. To this extent, the motivation for any actions which assist others to achieve happiness would be based upon an individualistic pursuit of personal satisfaction, even though the cumulative effect would be a general increase in the happiness of the group.

■ Mill, on the other hand, argued for an altruistic approach, emphasising that the search for happiness should be primarily based upon a consideration of the interests and welfare of others, rather than the interests of the individual. Those engaged in the creation and evaluation of the institutions and processes aimed at promoting happiness in society must ensure, as far as this is possible, that the interests of the individual are aligned with those of the group.

UTILITARIANISM AND THE SEARCH FOR HAPPINESS: JUSTICE v UTILITY

The place of justice in utilitarian theory

Bentham dismissed the notion of justice as a fantasy which was created for the purposes of convenience in the discussion of issues and situations which were the practical products of the application of the principle of utility. Mill believed that the idea of justice occupied a central place in the creation of a balance between social considerations of utility and individual concerns of liberty and equality. The notion of justice made it possible to create a balance which would have the effect of increasing happiness in society.

The relationship between justice and other social values

The notion of justice, for Mill, was closely tied in with his ideas on morality, equality and liberty. Justice implied the identification of interests which came together to form 'something which is not only right to do, and wrong not to do, but which some individual can claim from us as his moral right'. Equality of treatment is an essential element in the organisation of social life, and its contribution to the maximisation of happiness or satisfaction cannot be denied. Liberty helps to clarify the distinction and balance between the interests of the individual and the goals of society.

The scope of justice

According to Mill, the concept of justice has developed to cover many areas of activity which are not necessarily controlled through the agency of the law. In his view, justice must be seen as covering both constituted rights, which are regulated by the law, and other actions and claims which are not subject to law.

UTILITARIANISM AND THE POSITION OF THE INDIVIDUAL: LIBERTY v SOCIAL GOALS

The identification of liberty

In his essay, *On Liberty* (1859), Mill set himself the task of maximising the liberty of the individual. Within this general category, Mill included such specific freedoms as:

- liberty of expression and publication;
- liberty of thought and feeling;
- freedom of opinion;
- liberty of conscience;
- liberty of tastes and pursuits;
- liberty to unite for purposes which did not harm others.

The role of liberty in utilitarian theory

For Mill, liberty was an essential element in the pursuit of happiness, since it is only in a society where the specified freedoms are guaranteed that people will be content in the satisfaction that their individual interests are secured and that they need not fear that they may be arbitrarily sacrificed in one way or another for the purpose of the attainment of some social goal. According to Mill, the granting and the protection of these freedoms provided people with the ability of pursuing their own good in their own different ways, with the only limitation being that such pursuits should not interfere with the interests of others.

The idea of rights

In a way, for Mill, the idea of rights provides the distinction between the concept of liberty and the notion of justice. In his famous harm principle Mill states that:

> The only purpose for which power can rightfully be exercised over any member of a civilised community against his will is to prevent harm to others . . .

For Mill, the individual should have liberty in regard to actions which do not affect the rights of others. Such rights are determined by reference to justice. Justice defines that sphere of conduct where society has an overriding interest and the individual takes second place.

THE SECURITY OF LIBERTY IN UTILITARIAN THEORY

It is important to realise that, despite his argument in defence of liberty, Mill is still a committed utilitarian. To this extent, his ultimate aim is to provide for a standard or mechanism which will have the overall effect of maximising happiness or satisfaction in society. In this context, the pursuit of liberty can only be a means to an end. We guarantee certain liberties for the individual in order to make him/her relatively content in the knowledge that he/she is secure in respect to certain of his/her interests. Such contentment can only contribute to the sum total of social satisfactions. However, these liberties are not an end in themselves, and their provision takes second place to the overall purpose of attaining the social goal of happiness. In this case, therefore, where there is a danger that the individual exercise of the said liberties may lead to some unhappiness, as may occur when such exercise infringes on the interests of other persons, then it is perfectly acceptable to limit or extinguish those liberties. Freedom is therefore not absolutely secure in Mill's scheme of things, since it is ultimately only a means to an end.

Illustration: should criminal law uphold morality?

The conflict between utilitarianism and the harm principle is illustrated by ongoing debates on the question of the criminalisation of what some consider to be immoral behaviour, especially sexually deviant behaviour.

The Hart–Devlin debate

The relation between law and morality was raised in practical terms by the *Committee on Homosexual Offences and Prostitution in Great Britain.* This committee, headed by Sir John Wolfenden, investigated the legalisation of homosexuality and prostitution for three years. It issued its report in 1957, recommending the decriminalisation of homosexuality on the basis of freedom of choice and the privacy of morality. The Report took the view that immorality should not be law's concern. Hart and Law Lord-to-be Patrick Devlin contributed to the debate, engaging in a polemic now universally referred to as the Hart-Devlin debate.

Devlin: the majority rule

Devlin argued that the moral views of the majority, and the good of society, should prevail over the rights of the individual:

- Law without morality '... destroys freedom of conscience and is the paved road to tyranny'.

- Criminal law must preserve society's 'moral fabric' and so enforce moral norms to keep society from falling apart.

- Laws governing private morality guard against the disintegrating effects of actions that undermine the morality of society and so are justified.

- A shared morality is necessary for the survival of society.

- Immorality is what every right-minded person considered immoral. No acts are 'none of the law's business'.

Hart: individual rights

- Why should the conventional morality of some members of the population, be they the majority, be a justification for preventing people from doing what they want?

- J.S. Mill's harm principle.

■ Societies survive changes in basic moral views all the time; they do not disintegrate.

The Hart-Devlin debate was again relevant to the House of Lords decision in *R v Brown* [1993]. In this case the appellants belonged to a group of sado-masochistic homosexuals who over a 10-year period willingly participated in the commission of acts of violence against each other, including genital torture, for the sexual pleasure which it engendered in the giving and receiving of pain. It was held that consensual sado-masochistic homosexual encounters which occa-sioned actual bodily harm to the victim were offences against the person, notwithstanding the victim's consent, because public policy required that society be protected by criminal sanctions against a cult of violence which contained the danger of the proselytisation and corruption of young men and the potential for the infliction of serious injury. This case shows the limits of the harm principle: it is impossible to evaluate what is harmful independently of morality.

UTILITARIANISM AND THE ECONOMIC ANALYSIS OF LAW: THE ECONOMIC CONCEPTION OF JUSTICE

The approach which is generally known as the Economic Analysis of Law (EAL) has been put forward, particularly by American thinkers, as a viable alternative to classical utilitarianism. It generally seeks to avoid the problems that have confronted the latter theory by substituting different definitions and assump-tions in the argument for the maximisation of happiness or satisfaction. It does this especially by emphasising the *rationality* of persons and their desire for *efficiency* in the processes which lead to the achievement of individual and social goals.

In essence, this approach to questions of law and justice regards society as primarily an economic entity and people as being basically *homo economicus* – that is, humans are regarded as primarily economic agents, who act and react essentially for economic reasons, seeking as much as possible to maximise wealth and the satisfaction of their preferences. To this extent, the law becomes an economic tool, to be utilised efficiently for the maximisation of happiness. Its creation and application is governed by economic considerations. Justice then becomes an economic standard, based on the two elements of rationality and efficiency.

THE CONTRIBUTION OF THE ECONOMIC ANALYSIS OF LAW TO THE UTILITARIAN DEBATE

The case of the *felicific calculus*

One problem which has confronted classical utilitarian theory is the criticism that the *felicific calculus* developed by Jeremy Bentham for the prediction and measurement of human pains and pleasures is impracticable, since we cannot be certain whether people will be happy or not with any proposed act or measure. To answer this, EAL argues that human beings are rational animals. Being rational means that, where they are given a choice, people will choose and accept actions which they see as having the effect of maximising their satisfactions by giving them more of what they desire rather than less. Thus, we can easily predict what reactions people may have to a proposed act by simply measuring, in economic terms, how much people will get of what they desire from the proposed act.

The problem of predicting pleasures

Another problem for classical utilitarianism is the question of how to determine accurately exactly what people desire under a given situation. It is therefore difficult to decide upon what measures to take in order to maximise the happiness/satisfaction of the greatest number of people in society. EAL proposes an approach to the problem which reduces people's desires to economic units. A person's desire for a particular thing may be measured in terms of how much that person is prepared to pay for the thing, either in money or in the form of some other resource which they have available to them, such as time or effort. In this case, therefore, what a person wants is what they are willing to pay for, and the extent to which they want it is determined from the amount which they are willing to pay for it.

The question of balancing desires

Classical utilitarianism is criticised for seeking to balance the happiness of certain persons with the misery of other persons in society, and the argument is that this is not possible. EAL proposes a formula which, by determining people's desires and dislikes in economic terms, allows us to calculate the happiness or misery which a certain situation or action may cause by simply finding out how much certain persons will be willing to pay to have the action occur and how much other persons are willing to pay to have the situation or action not occur. In this way, the balance of pleasures and pains can accurately be discovered.

Contribution to legal thinking

EAL has proved very useful in legal thinking insofar as it offers pragmatic justifications or criticisms of legislation or legal decisions where doctrinal argumentation can prove unconvincing. For example, in the area of criminal law, if crime is considered to be a rational choice providing certain advantages, EAL can identify disincentives through a cost/benefit analysis.

RICHARD POSNER AND THE ECONOMICS OF JUSTICE

In his writings in two texts, *The Economic Analysis of Law* (1977) and *The Economics of Justice* (1981), Richard Posner articulates a theory of justice which generally equates justice with economic efficiency. His assumption is that the justice of social, political and legal arrangements can be determined in terms of the concept of wealth maximisation. In this regard, the operation of legal systems, in terms of the creation, application and enforcement of the law, and particularly the common law, can be understood and assessed in terms of economic efficiency. In *The Economic Analysis of Law*, Posner defines 'efficiency' as:

> ... exploiting economic resources in such a way that human satisfaction as measured by aggregate willingness to pay for goods and services is maximized.

Efficiency requires that society provide conditions in which the operation of the free market will ensure that goods, including certain rights and privileges, will be at the disposal of those who value them most highly and therefore those who are most willing to pay for them. To this extent, Posner, like the utilitarians, rejects the moral dimension of rights, and presents what is essentially an individualistic economic conception of justice.

Posner analyses the operation of the common law and, along with other proponents of EAL, concludes that law is basically a set of rules and sanctions which are intended for the regulation of the behaviour of persons whose primary instinct is to maximise the extent of their satisfactions, as measured in economic terms. The law is also administered by people, that is, lawyers and judges, whose main consideration is economic efficiency. Law is, therefore, created and applied primarily for the purpose of maximising overall social utility.

Posner further argues that in society, people will abide by the law if they predict that they will thereby reap greater economic benefits than they would get from the spoils of breaking such law. They will break the law if the opposite is true. People will take their disputes to court if the financial or economic benefits of such litigation will be greater than the economic burdens which will accrue.

In the same vein, judges adjudicate in disputes in the most economically efficient way possible. They punish the most economically destructive behaviour. They determine questions of liability, damages and compensation in ways which allocate resources to those who are most capable of putting them to efficient economic use, and they allocate rights to those who would be prepared to pay the most for them on the free market.

Posner makes favourable reference to the formula set out by Justice Learned Hand as a test for negligence in the case of *United States v Carroll Towing Company* [1947]:

> The defendant is guilty of negligence if the loss caused by the accident, multiplied by the probability of the accident's occurring, exceeds the burden of the precautions that the defendant might have taken to avert it.

For Posner, the common law has numerous examples of economic considerations being overtly taken into account in the operation of the law and the dispensing of justice. This can only be a sign that, even when it is couched in legal language, the question of justice is in fact an economic, rather than a legal or moral, standard.

Note

In 1959, the Wolfenden Committee Report recommended the legislation of homosexual acts between consenting adults as long as these were carried out in private. They also recommended the legislation of prostitution, as opposed to soliciting. The arguments justifying the Committee's conclusions were much the same as those set out by Mill in his argument for the maximisation of liberty, particularly the harm principle.

In regard to the harm principle, a problem is posed by the question of identifying exactly what is meant by 'harm'. Does this mean:

■ Physical tangible harm?

■ Physical harm and certain moral – that is, where there is a public dimension to a private act – harm?

■ Physical *and* moral harm?

In the context of the harm principle, Mill's reference to 'harm to others' may best be understood in the sense of 'harm to the interests of others'.

The liberty which people in society have in the pursuit of their own good in their own way must be limited by the need to protect the interests of others, for if it is not so limited then those whose interests are injured will be unhappy, thus reducing the general level of satisfaction in society. In society, some interests are left to the individual to decide on how best they may be protected or advanced. However, there are other interests which society will protect, either through express legal provision, or by way of tacit understanding in the form of public opinion. Such interests then constitute rights. Justice requires the protection of these rights and in this regard it is what justifies the limitation of the freedom or liberty of individuals.

You should now be confident that you would be able to tick all the boxes on the checklist at the beginning of this chapter. To check your knowledge of Utilitarianism why not visit the companion website and take the Multiple Choice Question test. Check your understanding of the terms and vocabulary used in this chapter with the flashcard glossary.

Rights

HOHFELD'S ANALYSIS OF RIGHTS

The question of what constitutes a right is a problematic one, since the word 'right' itself may mean a number of different things in different contexts, be they moral, political, economic or legal. The vocabulary of propositions and arguments about rights makes it difficult in many cases to distinguish between the specific connotations of the term, and this tends to obscure the meaning and value of rights as basic building blocks of law, as well as essential elements of the idea of justice. Wesley Newcomb Hohfeld (1879–1918), an American jurist, introduced theoretical elements in analytic thought in his analysis of rights – which he called 'the lowest common denominators of the law' – in several articles published posthumously in *Fundamental Legal Conceptions as Applied in Judicial Reasoning* (1919).

HOHFELD'S BASIC RIGHTS

Hohfeld's solution to the problem of defining rights was to clearly identify the basic legal conceptions which are usually described by the use of the term right, and then to distinguish between these conceptions by using very specific terms to express them. The idea was that speakers in a legal debate would have a coherent idea of the terms used by all by adopting the same meaning. This resulted in what is up to this day probably the most rigorous analysis of jural relations ever attempted. This analysis is of value in clarifying the implications of the term 'right' in various situations.

Hohfeld approached the problem through the process of defining these basic conceptions and then arranging them in pairs of opposites and correlatives, in order to distinguish between them. He identified eight different such conceptions, to which he attributed specific terms of description, and which he then rigorously defined. These were as follows:

1 *Right*: 'An enforceable claim to performance, action or forbearance by another.'
2 *Duty*: 'The legal relation of a person who is commanded by society to act or forbear for the benefit of another person either immediately or in the future, and who will be penalized by society for disobedience.'
3 *Privilege*: 'The legal relation of A to B when A (with respect to B) is free or at liberty to conduct himself in a certain manner as he pleases; when his conduct is not regulated for the benefit of B by the command of society, and when he is not threatened with any penalty for disobedience.'

4 *No-right*: 'The legal relation of a person in whose behalf society is not commanding some particular conduct or another.'

5 *Power*: 'The legal relation of A to B when A's own voluntary act will cause new legal relations either between B and A or between A and a third party.'

6 *Liability*: 'The relation of A to B when A may be brought into new legal relations by the voluntary act of B.'

7 *Immunity*: 'The relation of A to B when B has no legal power to affect one or more of the existing legal relations of A.'

8 *Disability*: 'The relation of A to B when by no voluntary act of his own can A extinguish one or more of the existing legal relations of B.'

Hohfeld proceeded to arrange these conceptions in terms of opposites and correlatives in order to illustrate clearly how they differed in terms of their legal implications and how in some cases they specifically contradicted each other. This arrangement may be represented in diagrammatic form as shown in the figure on the following page.

Hohfeld's analysis is based on a number of assumptions about the legal concepts and the relations which they describe:

■ There are four basic *rights*, that is:

● rights in the strict sense, which may also be called claim-rights;

● rights which are in fact liberties, or as Hohfeld calls them, privileges;

● rights which describe power, in the sense of the ability of one person to create or change legal relations with other persons; and, finally

● immunities, which are rights that protect a person from interference in a specific way by another person.

■ These basic rights are the lowest common denominator in all legal relationships, and any other rights which a person may claim to have can ultimately be reduced to a category of one of these four.

■ The Hohfeldian basic rights must be thought of as rights against a specific person, and they are distinguished from one another by reference to what they imply about the other party to a legal relationship. Each type of right represents one aspect of a legal relationship between at least two persons.

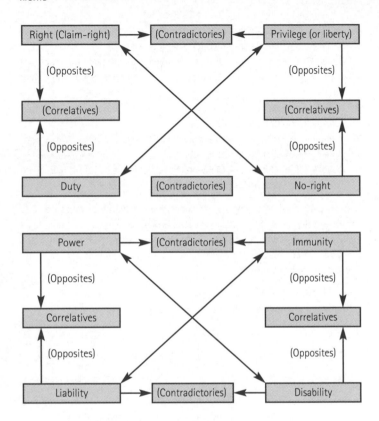

■ It is important to note that, although Hohfeld's analysis refers specifically to legal rights, the scheme of analysis can also be applied effectively to the investigation of moral rights.

The relationships between the basic rights and their counterparts can be explained as follows:

■ *Jural correlatives*: connected by vertical lines in the diagram – always exist together, so that where one person has, for example, a claim right, then another person must have a duty. Similarly, where one person has a power, another person must have a liability.

■ *Jural opposites*: connected by diagonal arrows in the diagram – can never be held by one person at the same time. So, a person who has an immunity in respect of certain subject matter cannot at the same time have a liability in respect of the same subject matter. In the same way, a person who holds a privilege or liberty with respect to a certain subject matter cannot simultaneously be the subject of a duty.

■ *Jural contradictories*: connected by horizontal arrows in the diagram – always imply that where one is held by one person, then another person lacks its contradictory. So, for example, the fact that A has a right to something, necessarily means that B does not have a privilege in respect of the same thing. Where B has a power in respect of the same subject matter, then C cannot at the same time have an immunity in respect of that particular subject matter.

JOHN RAWLS AND THE PRIORITY OF LIBERTY

'JUSTICE AS FAIRNESS'

Whereas the focus of John Rawls' work lies more on the idea of justice than on the notion of rights, still the introduction of Rawls' theory is relevant here, given the strict conceptual connection existing between justice and rights (at least in the dominant view). Rawls (1921–2002) set out most of his main ideas on justice in the text *A Theory of Justice* (1971), although he elaborated on these in subsequent other writings. In particular a restatement of his argument is presented in *Political Liberalism* (1993). His theory can be described as contractarian and libertarian, in that it regards society as being based on a social contract and in that it emphasises the liberty of the individual. Rawls regards the status and interests of the individual as being more important than the goals which a society may have and seek to achieve. It is for this reason that he is generally very critical of utilitarianism and other approaches to the question of justice which emphasise social goals at the expense of individual rights. Indeed, in *A Theory of Justice* (1971), Rawls sets out to articulate a set of principles of justice which, he argues, are superior to both classical and average utilitarianism in that they will accord better with both our intuitive and our considered moral judgments about what is just and what is not in respect of our position *vis-à-vis* social structures and their operation.

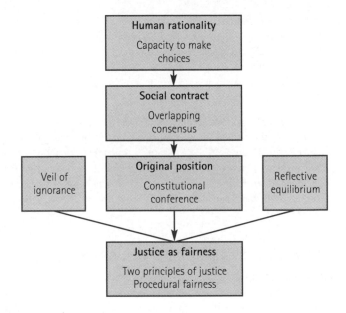

WHY JUSTICE AS FAIRNESS?

Rawls sought to reconcile the political ideals of equality and liberty. In his approach, Rawls emphasises the need for consent amongst the people who make up society to the principles which determine what is just and what is not in that society. He promotes the notion that society should be regarded as being based upon some sort of social contract or agreement, which then means that the individual is important in his/her own right, since it is by the choice of individuals that society comes into existence. It is the choice of the individual to join and remain in society, because of the benefits which can be derived from living together with other human beings. It is also the choice of the individuals to accept the burdens which become necessary in order for the community to be stable and viable.

At the same time, each person in society has an interest in ensuring that what they get out of this association, in terms of benefits and burdens, is their fair share. Because of this, it becomes necessary to ensure that the basic institutions of society – that is, those institutions which are responsible for distributing primary goods, such as material wealth, opportunities and other resources – must be structured in such a way that they are procedurally just. In other words, such institutions must operate in a manner which accords to each person what is probably their most important basic right in society – *the right to equal concern and respect*. The distribution of social benefits and burdens must be fair and must be seen to be fair in this sense – hence 'justice as fairness'.

THE PRIMARY SUBJECT OF JUSTICE

According to Rawls, the primary subject of justice – that is, the element which should concern us most when we consider issues relating to the creation of a just and well-ordered society – must be the basic structure of society. This is because the basic structure of society influences the existence of people in a fundamental way throughout their lives. The basic structure is made up of the main institutions which are involved in the distribution of the benefits and burdens of life in society. Such institutions include the entire set of major social, political, legal and economic institutions, such as, for example, the monogamous family, the constitution, the courts, private owner-ship of the means of production and competitive markets. The benefits of social life as made possible by social co-operation include the means of sustenance such as food and shelter. They also include other goods such as wealth and income, authority and power, as well as rights and liberties. These are what Rawls calls primary goods. The burdens of social life comprise certain liabilities, duties and obligations, such as, for example, the obligation to pay taxes.

Given the focus of questions of justice on the basic structure of society, Rawls argues that the main problem of justice, and the task facing those who would recommend ways of creating a just society or of redressing existing injustices, is one of articulating a set of principles which would ensure an accurate and concrete determination of what is just and unjust, as well as helping the development of policies which would assist in the correction of such injustices. Linked to this is the problem of ensuring that such principles are generally acceptable to the majority of people in society, so that there is consensus in the resolution of problems of injustice. Such principles would then become the basis for the creation of what Rawls refers to as a well-ordered society.

THE PROBLEM OF ESTABLISHING STANDARDS OF JUSTICE

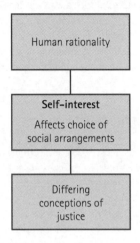

THE NATURE OF HUMAN BEINGS

Bentham and human sentience

Rawls disagrees with Bentham when, in setting out the theory of classical utilitarianism, the latter argued that the most important quality of human beings is their sentience, that is, the capacity to experience pain and pleasure. It was on this basis that Bentham argued for the pursuit and maximisation of pleasure and the reduction of pain for the greatest number of people in society. For Bentham and other utilitarians, the satisfaction of the desires of the majority in society takes precedence over the individual interests of particular people. Total or average utility is the goal, and, even if certain measures or arrangements may be painful for some, this is regarded as being necessary and appropriate, as long as the degree of happiness generated is greater than the misery caused. The goal of maximum social utility takes precedence over the rights and interests of individuals. The individual may be sacrificed for the greater good, for he or she is only a part of a bigger entity – society – and the satisfaction of his or her individual needs and preferences is only a means to an end.

Rawls and human rationality

For Rawls, the most important quality of human beings is not their sentience, but rather their rationality, that is, their ability to make choices. Humans have the ability to decide upon the goals which they want to pursue in life as individuals. They have the capacity to formulate coherent plans by which to achieve those goals, and they have the capability to utilise available resources in the most efficient manner to attain their chosen ends. Because of their rationality, human beings are characterised by self-interest, in the simple sense that, given a choice and all things being equal, a rational person would rather have more of a good thing than less.

The importance of choice

It is the capacity to make choices which makes the individual, as opposed to the community, so important in Rawls' view. Indeed, in thinking about society as being based upon a social contract, it would be difficult to see how societies could come into existence and continue to exist unless individual people choose to live in community with other persons. That choice would presumably be made on the basis that greater benefits might accrue from living within society than from living in isolation. This ability to choose must therefore be given a central place in any social arrangements, since it will ensure the continued stability of society.

The requirements for a well ordered society

A well ordered society must, for Rawls, be characterised by structures and institutions which permit maximum scope for the individual to make choices, to decide upon the goals which he or she wishes to pursue in life as an individual, and to formulate plans for the pursuit of such goals. The basic institutions of a well ordered society must also be structured in such a way that due consideration is given to the interests of individuals, and that the distribution of resources and opportunities is such that all persons in society get a fair allocation. Where resources are to be distributed unequally, then a well ordered society must ensure that those who are most disadvantaged are in a position ultimately to benefit from the overall distribution.

Utilitarianism v choice

For Rawls, it is only in a situation where individuals are capable of improving themselves under conditions of equality of opportunity that the rational person

99

may flourish. Utilitarianism creates conditions where the individual has little choice and has to accept what may be the arbitrary and unfair decisions of some central authority as to what should be done with scant resources. Whatever goals an individual may have for him/herself are ignored in the pursuit of overall utility. The rights and liberties which the person may have can be taken away or restricted in order to satisfy the preferences of some other persons or group of persons.

ESTABLISHING PRINCIPLES OF JUSTICE

The need for an overlapping consensus

One problem in the search for principles of justice is, according to Rawls, the problem of getting people to agree on the actual principles without being influenced by improper motives and considerations. This problem arises mainly because human beings are rational beings and are therefore self-interested. This self-interest tends to interfere with the making of impartial judgments as to what is acceptable and what is not. A person who is aware of his or her abilities or his or her social status will naturally tend to think in terms of what would be most beneficial to him or her given his or her advantages or disadvantages compared to the other members of society. Thus, a fairly well off person, economically, may not accept principles of justice which might require him or her to part with some of his or her wealth in order to improve the economic status of other, less well off persons. At the same time, these other persons may favour such principles, and yet they might find any arrangements which might further improve the position of the well off unacceptable. One requirement for consensus in the choice of principles of justice is, therefore, according to Rawls, the neutralisation of such negative self-interest. On the other hand, however, Rawls notes that human beings are not just rational, but they are also moral persons. In other words, they do have a sense of justice. People have an intuitive sense of what is just and what is not, and at the same time they are also capable of making considered moral judgments of what would constitute a just or unjust situation. This fact means that given the right conditions people are capable of making impartial decisions about principles of justice and this makes it possible to have what he calls an overlapping consensus regarding such principles.

The original position and the veil of ignorance

For Rawls, the right conditions for choosing principles of justice can be created by envisaging what he calls an 'original position'. This is a hypothetical construction which is similar to the situation which might have existed at the beginning of society, from the social contract point of view, when the founding fathers of society may have come together to decide what form their society was going to take and what structures were going to govern their community. Rawls invites us to imagine a similar sort of situation, which is, however, formally different in a number of respects, which are intended to ensure procedural fairness. Under such circumstances, one must then make a choice of principles of justice from a limited set of alternatives, working from one's intuitive sense of justice as well as one's considered moral judgments as to what is just.

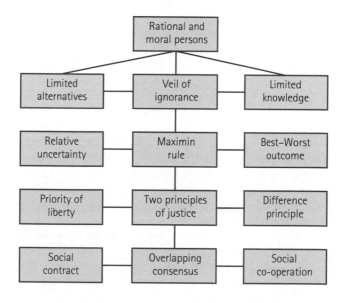

The main feature of the original position is the idea of the *veil of ignorance*. In this case, we imagine that the people who are to choose the principles of justice do not know anything about themselves or their situation other than that which is absolutely necessary to enable them to distinguish and to make a choice between the alternative sets of principles. The purpose of the veil of ignorance is to ensure that, in making their choice, the parties are not influenced by self-interest and that they make their decisions solely on the basis of general considerations.

The veil of ignorance makes it possible to have a consensus amongst people who may otherwise disagree with each other in the choice of principles purely for reasons of self-interest or selfishness. Given that the persons in the original position are moral, they will have a general sense of what is just and what is not. And, given that the same persons are rational, they will want to advance their own interests as much as possible. However, because they are generally ignorant of their particular circumstances, such people will not know which choice of principles will advance their interests in the best way. Under conditions of relative uncertainty, and all things being equal, a rational person will tend to choose an arrangement which will assure him or her of the best possible outcome. If an outcome is going to land him or her in the worst position, then the rational person will want that to be the most favourable worst position possible. This is what is called the *maximin rule*. Given the veil of ignorance, the rational and moral persons in the original position will be more likely than not to choose the same principles of justice. This is because they will know intuitively what is just, and because they will be aware that if they choose principles which might lead to, or perpetuate injustice then they themselves might end up suffering under an unjust arrangement. To choose anything other than principles which would ensure them the best worst position would be irrational. The veil of ignorance is therefore a most effective way of ensuring consensus.

Rawls' two principles of justice

Rawls proposes two principles of justice which he believes that people in the original position would choose and agree on. He argues that these principles accord with our most basic intuitions about justice and he contends that they should form the basis of any well ordered society. This means that these principles should govern the creation and operation of the institutions which make up the basic structure of society. In their operation, the principles therefore govern the distribution of primary goods in society. Rawls says that these principles should be lexically ordered, and that the first principle should be lexically prior to the second. What this means is that in every case, the requirements of the first principle should always be met to the fullest extent possible before any attempt is made to fulfil the requirements of the second principle.

The first principle: the principle of greatest equal liberty
Each person has an equal right to a fully adequate scheme of equal basic liberties which is compatible with a similar scheme of liberties for all.

This principle is concerned with the distribution of individual liberties as a subset of the total primary goods available in society. These liberties include:

- political liberty – that is, the right to vote and to be eligible for public office;

- freedom of speech and assembly;

- liberty of conscience and freedom of thought;

- freedom of the person along with the right to hold (personal) property;

- freedom from arbitrary arrest and seizure as defined by the concept of the rule of law.

The liberties should be enjoyed equally by all the citizens of a just society, since justice requires them to have the same basic rights.

The second principle
This principle regulates the distribution of other primary goods in society, including material wealth and social, economic and political opportunities. It determines the justice of such distribution in two different ways and is given as follows:

Social and economic inequalities are to be arranged so that they are both:

- to the greatest advantage of the least advantaged (that is, the representative worst-off person) – *the difference principle*;

- attached to offices and positions open to all under considerations of fair equality of opportunity – *the principle of fair equality of opportunity*.

Rawls' first lexical priority rule means that people in a just society must always be assured of their liberties before consideration is made of the distribution of material and other primary goods. Ultimately, this is to ensure that the element of choice, which enables people to define their own goals, to make up their own plans of life and to pursue such plans utilising the resources available to them without undue interference from society, is guaranteed. The priority of the first principle also requires that the basic liberty of citizens must not be restricted for the sake of greater material benefits for all, or even for the benefit of those least advantaged. There can be no trade-offs between liberty and material goods. This is what is referred to as the priority of liberty, for Rawls. Liberty may only be restricted for the sake of a greater liberty for all. Whenever a basic liberty is restricted, the effect of such restriction must be to create a more extensive system of liberty for everyone.

NOZICK AND THE THEORY OF ENTITLEMENTS

Robert Nozick (1938–2002) provides what is probably the most devastating attack on John Rawls' theory of justice as fairness, whilst setting out his own theory of justice. Nozick criticises Rawls' principles of justice for being based on what he regards as indefensible assumptions:

- that people's abilities are a common asset to be utilised for the good of all;

- that people are necessarily altruistic and that individuals will accept social arrangements and a system of distribution which will take from them some goods and redistribute those for the sake of providing the worst off members of society with certain advantages.

A further problem with Rawls' approach, for Nozick, is that the arrangements which will result from Rawls' two principles of justice would require unjustified and continuing interference with people's lives by a central authority intent on maintaining a particular pattern of distribution of goods.

Basically, Nozick is against all 'end state' theories of justice. For Nozick, theories of justice should not provide for the redistribution of social goods for the simple sake of achieving some centrally concocted conception of justice. What people have is a result of processes of acquisition which pre-date the stage at which any assessment of the justice or injustice of distribution is made. Approaches which simply have regard to the end state of these processes are therefore liable to be unjust because they do not take into account the history of present holdings of social goods.

Nozick puts forward a theory of entitlements, in which he argues that however unequal a distribution might be, it is to be regarded as just if the distribution came about through just steps from a previous distribution which was itself just.

A person is entitled to the social goods he holds if he came by such goods in a just manner, and such goods should not be taken away from him without justification. His notion of justice is that:

> A distribution is just if it arises from another just distribution by legitimate means ... Whatever arises from a just situation by just steps is itself just.

Nozick articulates three principles which he says would define the justice of holdings if the world were 'wholly just':

1 *The principle of justice in acquisition*: A person who acquires a holding in accordance with the principle of justice in acquisition is entitled to that holding.
2 *The principle of justice in transfer*: A person who acquires a holding in accordance with the principle of justice in transfer from someone else entitled to the holding is entitled to that holding.
3 *The principle of justice in rectification*: No one is entitled to a holding except by (repeated) applications of (1) and (2).

Correlated to the idea of entitlement to the fruits of one's labour and self-ownership is the idea of a 'nightwatchman' state. There is no justification for an extensive State mechanism whose operations may impinge upon individual entitlements and violate people's rights. Taxation and other coercive measures are justified only when they are instituted to uphold the minimal State. The taxation of some in order to meet the needs of others is equivalent to forced labour.

DWORKIN'S RIGHTS THESIS

THE RIGHTS THESIS

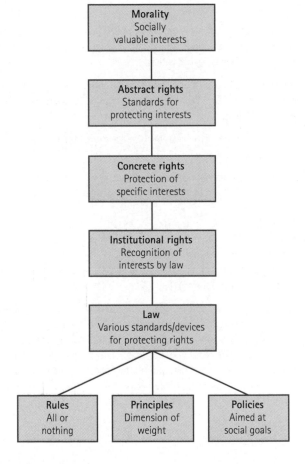

THE SOCIAL ORIGIN OF RIGHTS

Like Rawls, Dworkin believes that the specification and guaranteeing of the rights of individuals is a fundamental requirement for justice in society. Each person has an equal basic right to equal concern and respect. People are entitled to be accorded dignity and self-respect as individuals, since it is by their collective consent that social institutions come into existence and for their sake that those institutions operate in a certain way. For Dworkin, the rights of individuals arise, not from some metaphysical source, but from the social, political and legal institutions of the society in which they live. These rights express and protect certain interests which the majority of people in such a society commonly regard as valuable.

Society, for Dworkin, is generally a co-operative venture of individual persons whose outlook on the world is basically complementary. All persons have individual values and conceptions of the good. The reason why many individuals can live together in community is because such persons have a generally common world view, in that the interests and values which they hold as important are the same. When the members of a society generally agree on the value of certain interests, they tend to articulate such interests in the form of abstract rights, which they will then seek to protect by creating various institutions and the implementation of certain processes. In many societies, for instance, life, liberty, private property and human dignity are regarded as being valuable interests by individuals and by the majority of the members of such societies collectively. In those societies, then, you may find general or abstract rights to life, liberty, (private) property and certain rights pertaining to the protection and maintenance of self-respect, such as, for instance, a right to the protection of personal privacy. In most cases these rights are then institutionalised so that they become concrete rights, which the institutions of that society will be geared to protect. Certain standards are put in place to safeguard these rights. Such standards include rules of law and legal principles. Social policies may also be developed which tend to advance the welfare of the society's members generally and these may govern the processes of legislation and government. Legal rules and principles are used by judges during the adjudication of disputes to determine the rights of individuals and to determine the extent of individual liberty. These standards make up the 'moral fabric' of the society in question, since they are used to judge and to evaluate the justice or injustice of the social institutions in their operation.

THE LEGAL PROTECTION OF RIGHTS

The courts, for Dworkin, are extremely important vehicles for the articulation and safeguarding of the rights of individuals against undue interference by other social institutions in the pursuit of the wider goals of general welfare. The legislature in a particular society, for example, will have regard to matters of policy in creating arrangements for the general good. The implementation of these policies may have the effect of restricting the enjoyment of individual rights by certain members of society. Where such interference occurs, there is usually a dispute between the individual and the State or other groups of individuals regarding the extent of the individual's rights and the limits of social goals. In such a situation, it is then the role of the judge to determine what rights a person has and to ensure the institutional protection of such rights. Sometimes, these rights are clearly specified by clear rules of law, in which case the judge merely applies the rule to the facts and comes up with an answer. However, in some cases no rule of law will clearly apply, and the judge has to rely on principles in determining the disputed rights.

Principles and policies
Dworkin believes that, in making decisions on the basis of standards other than rules, judges should, and in fact do normally, rely on principles rather than on policies. He defines the distinction between principles and policies in the following way:

- *Principle*: He calls a 'principle' a standard that is to be observed, not because it will advance or secure an economic, political or social situation deemed desirable, but because it is a requirement of justice or fairness or some other dimension of morality.

- *Policy*: He calls a 'policy' that kind of standard that sets out a goal to be reached, generally an improvement in some economic, political or social feature of the community.

- *General distinction*: Principles are propositions that describe rights; policies are propositions that describe goals.

- *Distinction between a principle-based and a policy-based approach to justice*: Arguments of policy justify a political decision by showing that the decision advances or protects some collective goal of the community as a whole. The argument in favour of a subsidy for aircraft manufacturers, that the subsidy will protect national defence, is an argument of policy. Arguments of principle justify a political decision by showing that the decision respects or secures some individual or group right. The argument in favour of anti-discrimination statutes, that a minority has a right to equal respect and concern, is an argument of principle.

Rights as 'trumps'

For Dworkin, rights, as described by principles, are 'trumps' which serve to protect the individual against the encroachment of measures which seek to advance collective goals. To this extent, a right is a claim which an individual person can make that their interests be not sacrificed for the sake of the advancement of some social goal. The requirements of pragmatism and utilitarian considerations may sometimes mean that legislators will make decisions based on policies which are intended to secure some benefit, substantial or otherwise, for society generally. Such policies may require the sacrifice or at least a limitation of certain individual rights, including the general right to equal concern and respect. Justice requires that the courts should protect these rights and so principles must become the basis for judicial decisions in relevant situations.

For Dworkin, once a right has come into existence as a genuine right, then it can never be extinguished. In every case where there is a conflict between rights and social goals, the rights of individuals must take precedence. In this regard, Dworkin makes a distinction between 'strong rights', which cannot ever be extinguished or restricted, and other, weaker rights whose operation may in exceptional circumstances be restricted for the sake of some overwhelmingly beneficial goal which is in the general interest.

The example of reverse discrimination

Dworkin commented on the case of *The Regents of the University of California v Allan Bakke* [1978] in a series of three essays on reverse discrimination published in *A Matter of Principle* (1985). The *Bakke* case is a landmark case in America; it bars quota systems in college admissions but affirms the constitutionality of affirmative action programs. In this case a university set aside 16 places for disadvantaged minorities. Bakke, a white applicant, argued that had these 16 places not been kept open for minorities, he would have had a good chance of being admitted as his test scores were quite good. Bakke won his case and was admitted yet, on appeal, the constitutionality of affirmative action was affirmed by the U.S. Supreme Court.

Dworkin objected to Bakke gaining admission. For him, even if affirmative action rests on the use of 'racially explicit criteria', the long-term goal of affirmative action is to reduce the 'degree to which American society is overall a racially conscious society'. And 'no one in our society should suffer because he is a member of a group thought less worthy of respect than other groups.' Individuals have no right to prevent 'the most effective measures of securing [racial] justice from being used'. In other words, 'weak' individual rights, such as that of being admitted to a particular university, do not function as trumps in the face of compelling social goals such as achieving a society that would be less racially conscious.

You should now be confident that you would be able to tick all the boxes on the checklist at the beginning of this chapter. To check your knowledge of Rights why not visit the companion website and take the Multiple Choice Question test. Check your understanding of the terms and vocabulary used in this chapter with the flashcard glossary.

7

Theories of law and society

SOCIOLOGICAL JURISPRUDENCE, SOCIO-LEGAL STUDIES AND THE SOCIOLOGY OF LAW

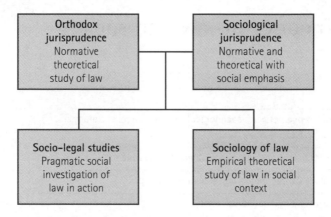

The contention here is that the pure, systematic analyses of law as a closed system carried out by most branches of jurisprudence can never produce a full understanding of the law because they do not take account of the social environment within which legal institutions exist. The fields of sociological jurisprudence, socio-legal studies and the sociology of law are distinct, though related, approaches to the investigation of the relationship between law and other social phenomena. The main link between them is to be found in the belief of scholars working within these schools of thought, in the role that a study of the workings of the various elements of society as a whole or specific combinations of them under certain circumstances has to play in the understanding of the more specific operations of the law as a distinct social phenomenon. The particular differences between these schools of thought are to be found in an analysis of the main social issues which they seek to investigate, and the approaches which they take in relating studies on the law to these issues.

SOCIOLOGICAL JURISPRUDENCE
Sociological jurisprudence is a juristic perspective that seeks to base legal arguments on sociological insights. It is an intrinsically *theoretical* approach to the study of the law grounded in empiricism. It specifically seeks to understand law

as a particular social phenomenon, in terms of how it comes into existence, how it operates and the effects that it has on those to whom it applies. To this extent, this school of law is very similar in its approach to the other, analytical schools of thought in jurisprudence, such as positivism. Its subject matter is the law proper. However, what distinguishes it from the other schools of jurisprudence is its methodology. Sociological jurisprudence seeks to examine closely the workings of society in general, in order to find therein the factors which determine the nature of law. In this regard, historically it has relied on the findings of social sciences such as sociology, as well as other social disciplines, including historical, political and economic studies, to help explain the nature of law.

Sociological jurisprudence has a long history, and can be said to have emerged with the realisation that a study of the various aspects of social life could assist in understanding the nature and workings of the law. Thus, its place in jurisprudential literature can be traced as far back as the writings of Hume who, in *A Treatise on Human Nature* (1740), argued that law owed its origin not to some quirk of human nature, but to social convention, and who described law as a developing social institution. Montesquieu, in *The Spirit of Laws* (1748), put forward the view that law originated in custom, local manners and the physical environment. He asserted that good laws were those which were in accordance with the *spirit of society*. Through the years, writers on the nature of society, such as Comte, Marx, Weber and Durkheim, have contributed to sociological jurisprudence, putting forward views on how various social phenomena influence the nature of law.

The close link between the theoretical study of the law on the one hand and the independent study of society on the other, has meant that sociological jurisprudence has been closely influenced by developments in the other social sciences, and its views on the nature of law have been progressively transformed. For this reason, it is difficult to point to any one proposition as being the central approach of this school of thought. However, there are certain assumptions which can be identified as characterising the thinking of almost all sociological jurists. The following are some of them:

■ Generally, there is a belief amongst sociological jurists that law is only one of a number of methods of social control. To this extent it is not unique in its function and place in society.

■ There is a general rejection of the notion that law is somehow a closed system of concepts, standards and structures and that it can stand on its own in its operation. Because there are certain problems which the law cannot resolve, it must therefore be seen as being open to modification through the influence of certain social factors. To this extent, sociological jurists reject what has been called a 'jurisprudence of concepts'.

▨ Sociological jurists tend to place more emphasis on the actual operation of the law – 'the law in action' – arguing that this is where the real nature of the law manifests itself, rather than in textbooks and other elementary sources.

▨ In discovering the building blocks of the law, sociological jurists disagree with the approach of the Natural Law school of thought, which proposes that there are certain sets of principles which describe absolute values and which then become or should be the basis of all law. Instead they take a relativistic approach, which regards law as being the product of a socially constructed reality. The basis of the law is to be found in the ways in which people in society regard their situation and their place in it and how society in general reacts to the problems confronting it.

▨ There is a general interest in utilising the findings of the sociological sciences in understanding the nature of law and thus to make law a more effective tool for social justice.

Views differ, however, as to what constitutes social justice and how best this may be achieved.

The following are some examples of thinkers who have contributed to sociological jurisprudence.

RUDOLF VON JHERING (1818–92): GERMAN LEGAL SCHOLAR

Generally credited with being the father of sociological jurisprudence, Jhering defined law as:

> ... the sum of the conditions of social life in the widest sense of the term, as secured by the power of the State through the means of external compulsion.

Jhering took up the utilitarian principles of Jeremy Bentham and used them as a basis for the argument that law existed to serve the social interest. The law was to be seen as a coercive instrument which existed to resolve conflicts which might arise between the interests of individuals and the interests of society as a whole. In these circumstances, the common interests of all members of society took precedence over the interests of particular members. The law could not be applied mechanically because it had to operate effectively to ensure social utility.

MAX WEBER (1864–1920): GERMAN SOCIOLOGIST AND ECONOMIST

Max Weber regarded the sociology of law as being central to general sociological theory. He was the first to try to provide a systematic sociology of law, and in doing this he sought to understand the development and workings of Western capitalist society. Weber engaged in historical and comparative studies of the major civilisations in the world as he tried to understand two main features of Western society, that is, capitalism as an institution and rationalism in the legal order. He saw law as going through three 'ideal' stages of development:

- *Charismatic*: where legality arises from charismatic revelation – that is, as a gift of grace – through 'law prophets', who are rulers believed to have extraordinary personal qualities. The law which they propound is supported by an administrative apparatus of close aides or 'disciples'.

- *Traditional*: where charisma may be institutionalised through descent and the law-making powers pass to a successor. Law is then supported by tradition and inherited status, as in the case of new monarchies.

- *Rational*: where there is a 'systematic elaboration of law and professionalised administration of justice by persons who have received their legal training in a learned and formally logical manner'. In this case, the authority of law is based on the accepted legitimacy of the law givers, rather than on charisma. There is a rationalised legal order which dominates in an impersonal fashion.

According to Weber, the rationality of law in Western societies is a result of the rationalism of Western culture. This legal rationalism is the product of a number of factors. Economic forces have played a significant but not necessarily a pivotal role. Capitalism provided the conditions under which rational legal techniques, once developed, could spread. Institutions of the capitalist system are predicated upon calculation and to this extent they require a 'calculable legal system' which can be rationally predicted. The growth of bureaucracy established a foundation for the systematisation of the administration of rational law. Legal professionals have also contributed to rationalisation. Indeed, Weber regarded English lawyers, with their vested interest in the retention of the anachronistic formalism of the English legal system, as a major impediment to rationalisation of the law in this country.

ÉMILE DURKHEIM (1858–1917): FRENCH SOCIOLOGIST

Durkheim wrote on legal issues ranging from the criminal process to the law of contract. Methodologically, Durkheim was a functionalist, which means that he analysed social facts in terms of the function they fulfilled for the survival of society as a whole. As such, the main function of law is to generate social solidarity.

He made a distinction between two types of such social solidarity or cohesion:

- *Mechanical solidarity*: which he said was to be found in small scale homogeneous societies. Here, he believed, most law would be of a penal and repressive nature, since the entirety of society would take an interest in criminal activity and would seek to repress and deter it.

- *Organic solidarity*: to be found in more heterogeneous and differentiated societies where there is a greater division of labour. In such societies there is less of a common societal reaction to crime and the law becomes less repressive and more restitutive.

Durkheim also believed that crime was a normal occurrence in any society. He even thought that crime fulfilled useful functions as the collective expression of outrage reinforces the social reality of the moral order, and this strengthens the solidarity of the collective. Violation of norms weakens the social bond by undermining the universality of the norms that bind a society. Punishment reaffirms the universal character of the norms. So the social function of punishment is to reinforce the norm. Crime and punishment work together: crime violates norms which are reinforced by punishment, which reasserts the sacred moral order.

ROSCOE POUND (1870–1964): AMERICAN JURIST

Pound set out what may be described as an intrinsically American sociological jurisprudence, in which he treated jurisprudence pragmatically, as an instrument of social technology to be utilised in resolving problems of the satisfaction of competing social claims and the resolution of conflicts in the distribution of social goods. Pound took an instrumental view of law, with legal rules prescribed 'to further social ends'.

The various claims and interests can be discovered through an analysis of social data. Such claims and interests exist independently of the law and it is the function of the law to serve and reconcile them for the good of society as a whole. In this regard, Pound saw society as being static, cohesive and wholly homogeneous, with its members sharing traditions and values. In this case, the operation of law would be within an atmosphere of general consensus.

SOCIO-LEGAL STUDIES

This is an approach to the question of law and society which has in recent years almost completely overwhelmed the field which has traditionally been occupied by sociological jurisprudence. Socio-legal studies, as a discipline, differs from sociological jurisprudence in that it does not have any specifically theoretical underpinning. Unlike the latter, which seeks to provide an analytical conception of the idea of law by looking at other social phenomena, the field of socio-legal studies is more concerned with pragmatic issues of how best to make the law, in its various aspects, work more effectively to achieve specific goals, usually identified with the idea of the rule of law or some notion of justice.

Scholars in socio-legal studies are generally not concerned with explaining the nature of law or its place in society or in relation to the State. There is a general acceptance of the legal system in its essence as being a central element of social life whose position in regard to other social institutions and the State is essentially unproblematic. They instead advocate the recognition of law in its accepted social context, emphasising an empirical approach to the problems raised by the operation of the legal system and reform-orientated research which looks more to the 'law in action' than the 'law in the books'.

THE SOCIOLOGY OF LAW

This field of legal study has gained precedence particularly in the last 35 years. It is different from sociological jurisprudence in its approach to the question of law and society, both in terms of its ideology and its methodology. Whereas sociological jurisprudence sought to provide an understanding of the *nature of law* through certain social phenomena, the sociology of law seeks to explain the *nature of society* from an investigation of the law as a form of social control. For example, on the basis of recent developments in criminal law involving today intensive surveillance mechanisms, many scholars argue that we live in a culture of control. The nature of our laws allows us to diagnose the kind of society we live in.

THE MARXIST ACCOUNT OF LAW AND SOCIETY

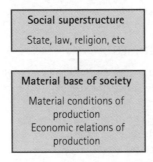

The initial proponents of Marxist theory were Karl Marx (1818–83), Friedrich Engels (1820–95) and Vladimir Lenin (1870–1924). The Marxist school of thought is a comprehensive system of thought, covering, among other things, the areas of sociology, history, politics and economics. Specific Marxian writings on law have generally been rather sparse. This is because of the secondary place that law and other elements of what Marxists regard as the social superstructure have been allocated in Marxist theory.

Materialism – base and superstructure

Marxist theory is materialist, which means that the material conditions of life – economic, physical, environmental – are the most important factors in society. Marx and Engels use the base-superstructure metaphor. The base consists of the relations of production – work conditions, the division of labour, and ownership of means of production – which people enter into to produce the necessary commodities of life. These relations fundamentally determine society's other relationships and ideas, and condition the superstructure. Yet, their relation is *not* strictly causal, because the superstructure often influences the base; however the role of the base in determining the superstructure is dominant. For example, the shift away from agriculture to mass industrialisation leads to a change in political models of government.

MARXIST HISTORICAL MATERIALISM – THE HISTORICAL DEVELOPMENT OF ECONOMIC RELATIONS OF PRODUCTION
See diagram overleaf (p 120).

Marxist thought is also characterised by *economic determinism*, since it argues that the development of society from one stage to the next is inevitable, and that it is the changes in the economic environment, with changes in the relations of production, which dictate the rate of social development. Marxist ideas on social development thus place much emphasis on the historical stages through which human society has gone, seeking to demonstrate that the transition from one stage to another is inevitable, and that such transition is directly linked to a transformation of the material base of society. This is what constitutes the historical materialist conception of society and law within the Marxist school of thought. There are supposed to be six main stages of development – or modes of production – through which societies are supposed to go.

1 Primitive communalism
This is the earliest stage of society, when people have just come together to live in specific communities. The mode of production is characterised by a communal effort in the production of the means of sustenance, since technology is relatively rudimentary and there is no distinctive division of labour. The *means of production* – that is, the main natural and other resources from which something of value may be extracted, for example, land – are communally owned, if at all, and everybody gets the full value of the labour which they put into production, since there are no employers and employees. At this stage, there is little need for centralised regulation of social or economic activity, and so specific administrative institutions, such as the State or law, do not exist. Social control is through communal morality and social pressure. However, at some stage, certain contradictions start to occur within this society. These contradictions arise primarily as a result of the accumulation of personal property. With the development of the *forces of production*, such as, for instance, the technological improvement of the *instruments of labour*, it becomes possible to

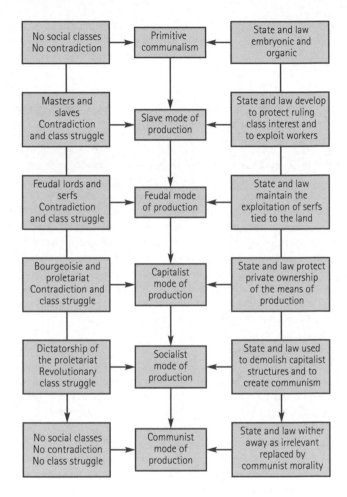

produce more, and in this situation some persons begin to acquire a surplus of the wealth extracted from the basic means of production. Inequalities between individuals and groups begin to appear. There is a division of labour as people diversify in the search for more rewarding occupations. People who have acquired wealth will seek to acquire even more through employing the labour of others. This is the beginning of the division of society into classes which are primarily antagonistic towards each other. A section of the community will gradually and inevitably acquire control of the means of production, whilst the rest are made to work with little or no reward for their labour. The State arises under these conditions as an instrument by which the owners of the means of production will seek to maintain their exploitation of the dispossessed who are then kept in a state of subservience through the use of law and other social institutions which arise or are created specifically to protect the interests of the owners of the means of production, who then become the ruling class. The State and law are thus the direct products of the economic relations of production, where there is a division of labour, the demarcation of society into classes with contradictory interests, and inequalities in the benefits which people get from the fruits of their labour.

2 Slave mode of production

The contradictions which arise in primitive communalist society due to changes in the economic relations of production will inevitably come to a head when the State and law are strengthened to the extent where the ruling classes can control, not just the labour of the oppressed classes, but their very lives. It becomes necessary in this case to institute social arrangements which have the ultimate effect of denying the oppressed classes their very individuality and humanity, turning them into chattels at the disposal of the owners of the means of production. This heralds the advent of the slave mode of production, where social, political and legal institutions are used directly to confirm and protect the *status quo*. Laws in this mode of production have the specific function of keeping the slaves under control, protecting the interests of the slave masters, and ensuring the continuation of the relations of production. The State also exists primarily for this purpose. However, it is inevitable that there will be a *class struggle*. The chained masses cannot remain subservient forever, and slave riots, etc., will begin to affect production. Eventually, it will become counterproductive for the ruling classes to maintain the economic relations of production which underpin the slave mode of production. The contradictions characterising this mode will eventually resolve themselves in a loosening of the control which the ruling classes have over their slaves and this paves the way to a newer and qualitatively different mode of production.

3 Feudal mode of production

In this mode of production, the oppressed classes are still exploited, but they cease to be the direct property of the ruling classes. They are given relative freedom, and some access to the means of production, through being allowed certain property; for example, they are given portions of land to farm. However, they are still tied to the feudal lords, who are still the ruling class and who still control the means of production. Serfs are attached to the land, and have to hand over a portion of what they produce to the feudal lord. The lord thus gains the surplus value of the labour of the serfs. There is still a class division in society, and the class struggle continues. The State and law of the feudal mode of production reflect the existing economic relations of production and are geared towards protecting the interests of the ruling classes. There are still contradictions which will push society to move on to another mode of production.

4 Capitalist mode of production

In the capitalist mode of production, the serfs are unshackled from the land and from their social and political masters. They have relative freedom of movement and are capable of owning some personal property. However, this freedom serves simply to enable the oppressed classes to be at liberty to sell their labour for a wage, which is of less value than the actual value of the labour which they put in. The ruling classes, now capitalists, have no responsibility for the welfare of the working classes since the latter are at *liberty* to roam around and sell their labour on the market. Yet, the capitalist class still own the means of production and they appropriate the surplus value, which is the difference between the actual value of the labour which the working classes put into production, and the value of the wage which they receive for working. Under these circumstances, the working classes – *the proletariat* – are naturally antagonistic towards the capitalist class – *the bourgeoisie* – and the class struggle continues. As before, the State and law are instruments by which the ruling classes keep the oppressed classes under control. The existing exploitative economic relations of production are maintained and protected through a number of social, economic, political and legal devices. The fallacy is perpetuated, and the working class is persuaded by various means to accept it, that all individuals in society are actually free, that the political system is liberal and democratic and therefore one which looks after the interests of all, and that private property is the highest and most appropriate expression of each person's humanity and individuality. Laws are promulgated which protect personal property, and the courts are supposed to protect individual rights and liberties. However, the only people who have property, rights and liberties worth protecting are members of the ruling class. The law and State are again merely the instruments of exploitation, expressing, securing and maintaining the economic relations of production. Contradictions are at their deepest in capitalist society and the class struggle reaches a stage where it has to be resolved in some sort of revolutionary upheaval.

5 Socialist mode of production

The socialist mode of production is brought about through a revolution of the proletariat, in which they overthrow the bourgeoisie ruling class and establish a dictatorship of the proletariat. This is a transitional stage in which the working class, who are now the ruling class, use the power and institutions of the bourgeoisic State to transform the capitalist economic relations of production. Private property is abolished, the means of production are placed under communal ownership and capitalist institutions are demolished. In the socialist mode of production, the State and law are fairly strong, since these are the weapons by which the proletariat will dismantle the bourgeoisie superstructure and create new relations of production, where those who work get the appropriate value of their labour.

6 Communist mode of production

The ultimate goal of the dictatorship of the proletariat is to create a classless society, where there are no inequities in access to the means of production. Such a classless society is described by the Communist mode of production. Because there are no classes, there will be no class struggle. Because most people are relatively satisfied there will be no criminal or other antisocial activities which characterise the capitalist mode of production. Because the economic relations of production are not exploitative, there are no contradictions in society. Under these circumstances, there will neither be a need of the State nor of law. Such institutions will therefore wither away. Conflicts between individuals, which will inevitably arise, will subsequently be resolved through the operation of an emerging public Communist morality.

MARXIST DIALECTICAL MATERIALISM

(See also p. 7). The historical development of society, described above, is regarded by Marxist theory as inevitable. Marxists regard irreconcilable contradictions as inherent in all modes of production prior to the establishment of

Communist society. These contradictions are a result of the division of society into classes and exploitative relations of production. The contradictions are reflected in the ongoing class struggle.

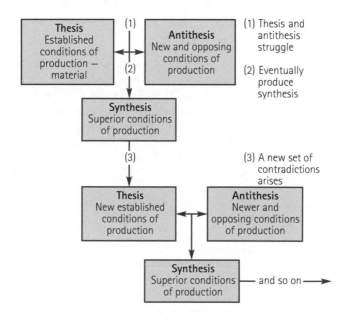

The idea of contradictions in the material base of society and their inevitable resolution through transition to a newer and 'higher' mode of production with different relations of production is the linchpin of Marxist social and legal theory. It is based on the notion of the dialectic, first established by the German philosopher, Hegel, and later adopted by Marx. Hegel believed that the basis of all social development was the contradiction between ideas – between a thesis (established idea) and an antithesis (opposing idea) – whose resolution would lead to the establishment of a newer and higher idea – the synthesis – which in turn would be challenged by a different antithesis.

Marx adopted the Hegelian dialectic and, as he said, 'turned it on its head'. Instead of being the motor of social development, ideas simply became the expression or reflection of such development. The development itself was based on changes within the material conditions of social life – particularly the economic relations of production. This material base underwent changes arising from contradictions within itself, and these had little to do with ideas. In each mode of production was to be found a thesis, consisting of the established relations of production. This would be challenged by an antithesis, comprised of elements of the class struggle. The result would be a different set of relations of production, which would herald the dawn of a new mode of production. In all this, the State, law and other institutions have little influence except as instruments in the hands of the ruling class to be used to protect their own interests. These institutions are neither self-supporting nor autonomous. They are merely part of a superstructure – a flimsy covering for the actual factors determining social development.

EVGENY PASHUKANIS' MARXIST INTERPRETATION OF LAW (1891–1937)

The Soviet jurist Pashukanis applied Marx's ideas to legal theory. *Law and Marxism* was written shortly after the October Revolution, still in the heyday of communism. It contains fairly revolutionary ideals.

Pashukanis' account is more ideologically informed than economically oriented: our law is bourgeois law centred on a mythical, free-willing individual, and in fact is an instrument of class domination (by protecting the property rights of the dominant class as well as the social and moral structures which support them). The supposed neutrality of law is a myth, for the very form of law in capitalist societies reflects the fact that legal subjects are primarily conceived as property owners.

Pashukanis argues, after Marx, that all creative processes are seen in terms of commodities (i.e. can be bought and sold and so have a value as commodity, including labour). Therefore, individuals relate to each other as property owners (of labour, means of production etc.) and the law reflects that because it protects primarily the freedom of market transactions. Further, legal subjects are seen in terms of individual rights and duties, as equals. Real differences in the material conditions of existence of different people are glossed over as irrelevant to law.

In the same way, criminal law is primarily designed to protect class interests.

> The would-be theories of criminal law which derive the principles of penal policy from the interests of society as a whole are conscious or

unconscious distortions of reality. 'Society as a whole' does not exist, except in the fantasies of jurists. In reality we are faced only with classes, with contradictory, conflicting interests.

For Pashukanis, law is thus an ideological instrument in the hands of the dominant classes. And a successful legal system is a system where people do not notice that its primary function is to perpetuate class domination.

MARXISM TODAY

Marx's vision of the end of the private ownership of the means of production – and so of capitalism – as the natural outcome of human history, which was to be achieved after a necessary period of dictatorship by the proletariat, started losing credit in most Western countries when the reality of communist regimes started to seep through to the West. By the time Mao's Cultural Revolution peaked in China in 1968, leading to the verbal and physical abuse of the 'bourgeoisie' and resulting in many deaths, most European intellectuals and activists had severed their connections with communism-inspired politics. In the UK the final blow to the credibility of Marx's political economy came with the collective movements of the 1980s (such as the miners' strike), movements whose ultimate failure highlighted the weakness of organised labour and so the vacuity of the Marxist promise of a classless society.

Yet, if socialism ceased to incarnate a plausible future for mankind some time in the 1980s, Marxist thought retains its importance as a critical tool to this day. Thus in the UK, by the mid-1970s Marx's conceptualisation of society in terms of power-relations provided the theoretical framework for all critical inquiries into the nature of law, power and authority, with narratives of oppression and domination proliferating as means of problematising the status quo (e.g. feminism, anti-psychiatry, discourses on race, colonisation, criminality, poverty and so on). And even today, though there are few bona fide Marxists left, there certainly lingers, in most left-leaning theoretical work, a tendency to interpret 'reality' in terms of oppressed/oppressor dichotomies.

In fact Marx's theoretical influence in the 1970s and 1980s was matched only by that of Sigmund Freud, probably because of the fundamental challenge embodied by both thinkers to the idea of society as a benevolent and progressive edifice. Indeed for Marx, human societies are structured by relations of exploitation and oppression, with the State cast as the primary instrument of domination. For Freud, the repression of desire is both a precondition to, and an effect of, civilisation (*Civilisation and its Discontents*, 1929). It is perhaps only with the work of Michel Foucault (see Chapter 9) that these – admittedly over-simplistic – interpretations of the Marxist and Freudian theories started to be themselves truly problematised.

You should now be confident that you would be able to tick all the boxes on the checklist at the beginning of this chapter. To check your knowledge of Theories of law and society why not visit the companion website and take the Multiple Choice Question test. Check your understanding of the terms and vocabulary used in this chapter with the flashcard glossary.

8

Feminist legal theory

ORIGINS AND AIMS OF FEMINIST LEGAL THEORY

The basic starting point of feminist legal theory is the belief that law essentially reflects the view of men, who have made the law to suit their representation of reality. Thus it is often said that law is 'patriarchal', favouring masculine values and concerns.

Patriarchy

- Refers to the structuring of families around the figure of the father.

- The father is endowed with primary authority over other family members.

- By extension, patriarchy refers to a model of social organisation in which men take primary responsibility for all functions of authority.

- In such models men are the dominant figures in all fields of decision-making: social, economic, political, legal.

Most forms of feminism challenge patriarchy as an unjust social system that is oppressive to women.

One of the consequences of law being man-made is that the concerns of women are often overlooked or trivialised. The low conviction rate in rape cases and the question of domestic violence are cases in point.

Feminist legal theory explores the theoretical issues arising from the relationship between women and law, with the aim of moving towards a system in which women (as well as men) are treated fairly in society. Feminist legal theory is therefore subversive: it aims to change society. The term 'feminism' sometimes mistakenly conjures up an image of 'manhaters' rather than women (and men) who merely object to the treatment of women as second-class citizens.

- Feminists want justice rather than the domination of one sex over the other.

- Unlike jurisprudence, feminist legal theory is therefore rooted in political activism.

- The feminist movement has struggled for women's equality and freedom at different points in history, whenever women have refused to be downtrodden.

- For this reason, the feminist movement has much in common with anti-racist movements.

The law has historically played a role in women's oppression. For example, under the 'doctrine of coverture' married women were not even viewed as 'persons' in law and therefore could not own property or sue or be sued in the courts. It was legal for husbands to beat their wives. There were a number of cases in which women challenged their position in the courts, culminating in the Persons Case: *Edwards v Attorney General* [1929] AC 124, in which it was finally conceded that women were to be classified as persons. Afterwards, the press congratulated women on the progress they were making.

This is a useful lesson about the common law. Rather than recognising that the court was forced to overturn a legal precedent (that women were not to be classified as 'persons') as a result of the political achievements of the suffragettes, the papers pretended that the law had always been correct. Women were treated as if they had just been transformed into 'persons', instead of simply overturning oppressive laws. Similarly, women fought to be accepted as lawyers and judges, not only to be able to vote but to be in Parliament and to be respected in daily life. Note that this raises theoretical issues about what it means to be a 'person', the law's claim to define us and how the common law operates (for an accessible introduction to this history, see the classic: A Sachs and JH Wilson, *Sexism and the Law: A Study of Male Beliefs and Judicial Bias*, Oxford: Martin Robertson, 1978).

Today in the West, women's position has vastly improved from the days of the doctrine of coverture. However, feminists point out that there are still inequalities in the UK. Women's pay continues to be lower than men's despite the Equal Pay Act 1970. Women still end up working a 'double day': taking on more work within the home than men, alongside paid employment. They end up with more menial roles, both in the workplace and the home, and are subject to more negative stereotypes: for example, there are still some sexual double standards, with women treated more harshly than men for enjoying sex.

Feminists claim both freedom and equality for women. Feminist legal theorists are interested in how these terms can be understood. They are also concerned as to how the subordination of women overlaps with other forms of subordination, for example on the grounds of race, sexuality or disability. What perpetuates different inequalities? No feminist legal theorist is likely to argue that sexism is the only area of subordination. They see the struggle for a fairer society as including other areas in which people are positioned as second class or exploited. There are a number of central theoretical problems that have been raised by feminist legal theory. The most important debates will be discussed in turn.

EQUALITY/DIFFERENCE DEBATE

There has been much discussion of this problem within feminist legal theory. The problem is historical and expresses a dilemma faced by feminists. Societies have often tried to justify treating women as second class on the grounds that they are *different* from men. The ways in which they have been viewed as different have changed historically – showing how inconsistent sexist arguments against women can be. So, for example, when the ability to think (or to use reason) became viewed as important then women were stereotyped as being irrational. However, when, at a different time, sentiment was prioritised women were viewed as too rational!

How have women responded? They have often argued that they should have *the same* legal rights as men because they are basically *the same* as men, that they are equally rational, for example. This is the 'equality' argument. This seems fair enough, but there are some areas in which women and men do differ. The extent to which this is the case is contentious, but it is clear that the experience of pregnancy is at least one example. If women are to be treated exactly the same as men, then how should pregnant women be treated?

A practical legal example can illustrate this argument. Initially, employers argued that to sack a woman on the grounds that she was pregnant could not be classed as sex discrimination because there could be no pregnant male to compare a woman's situation with. Later the courts compared the employer's treatment of pregnant women with that of sick men. It was only later that the sacking of a woman on the grounds that she was pregnant became classed as sex discrimination *per se*. Some feminist legal theorists argue that women should not have to ground their claim for justice on having to prove that they are exactly the same as men. This is the 'difference' argument.

The problem for the 'difference' argument is that it can be seen as playing into the hands of those who want to see women's freedom restricted on the grounds of their sex. Just as arguments about racial difference have been used to try to justify racism, so an emphasis upon sexual difference has been used to try to excuse sexism.

There have been different ways of dealing with the equality/difference problem. For example, Drucilla Cornell has argued that, instead of claiming equality with men (which involves comparing women with men), women should base their claims upon the freedom to define themselves as persons. She suggests a broad legal test that derives from philosophical principles: that when judges decide a case they should consider whether 'free and equal persons would agree'.

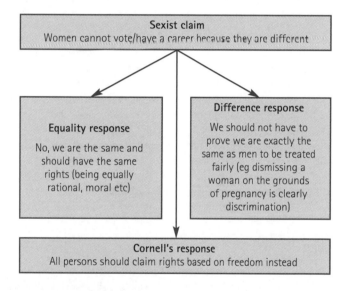

Sexist claim
Women cannot vote/have a career because they are different

Equality response
No, we are the same and should have the same rights (being equally rational, moral etc)

Difference response
We should not have to prove we are exactly the same as men to be treated fairly (eg dismissing a woman on the grounds of pregnancy is clearly discrimination)

Cornell's response
All persons should claim rights based on freedom instead

PUBLIC/PRIVATE DIVIDE

Care must be taken not to confuse this distinction with the relationship between public law (involving the State) and private law (in which the litigants are individuals or companies). When feminists talk about the 'private realm', in this context, they mean 'the household', and 'public' refers to everything else, including what happens in the workplace and in government.

Why is the public/private divide important for feminist legal theory? Some societies, at different times, have tried to restrict women to work within the home and to view them as outside of public life, hence stopping them from having a voice in democratic decisions or even a career. Some political/legal theorists have therefore ignored women's subordination and exploitation, viewing it as something 'private' that should not be the concern of the law. This has been linked with a similar view that what happens to women in the home is somehow 'natural' rather than a political issue. This is analogous to the way racists have tried to justify racial discrimination by claiming that ethnic minority people are somehow 'naturally' inferior, hence better suited to certain jobs. Here, sexists try to argue that women's position in the family is 'natural' despite the fact that the 'family' has taken different forms in different cultures.

The public/private divide has been detrimental to women because it has allowed behaviour that would usually be viewed as a crime, such as domestic violence, to go unpunished. In other words, by viewing wife-beating as 'private' it was not subject to regulation by law. It is only because of protests from feminists that the police are now expected to treat domestic violence as a serious issue. One of the important slogans of the 1960s' feminist movement, 'the personal is political', captures this important point. Feminists argued that 'politics' is not simply about what happens in government but concerns all acts of power, including the way in which women are treated in everyday life. In this way feminist legal theorists recognised that women were not demeaned or constrained because of some personal or natural characteristics but because of the way in which society was organised. It was therefore possible to change it.

POWER

Just as feminist legal theorists have argued that the treatment of women in the home is political, they have also examined the meaning of 'power'. In this area, feminist concerns have dovetailed with contemporary continental philosophy. It is necessary to think carefully about this point. A traditional view of politics was that 'politics' described acts performed by government: the passing of laws, the workings of the institutions of State. Power was viewed as being held by the government. Feminists have argued that the term 'political' applies to all areas of life in which some people have power over others and in which there are struggles for freedom from oppression. (It is worth noting that the recognition that husbands have traditionally had power over wives is not new. Historically, if a wife killed her husband it was legally classed as a type of treason!)

Recently, some feminist legal theorists have built on the work of the influential philosopher, Michel Foucault (1926–84). Foucault traced the operation of 'micro-processes of power' (mundane operations of power in everyday life) in ways that fitted with feminist analyses of power which also focused upon everyday power struggles (see Critical Legal Studies).

THE 'REASONABLE MAN/PERSON'

In tort law, the test for breach of duty in negligence is that the defendant has fallen below the standard of the 'reasonable man'. This has been updated to refer to the 'reasonable person' but this change of vocabulary does not address a problem raised by feminist legal theorists. They have pointed out that the 'reasonable person' test assumes that there is only one view in society as to what should be classed as reasonable behaviour. Most of the time we may all agree. The problem arises in situations when views as to what amounts to reasonable behaviour differ according to whether one is a man or a woman. For example, there was a time when men viewed some behaviour as 'just a joke' which most people would now classify as sexual harassment. There has been a cultural change as to what is acceptable behaviour. Before this change in attitudes, men and women would have different views as to what was reasonable behaviour. This may still be the case, because women are conscious that some sexual behaviour by men may escalate and they may feel threatened by a man's sexual comments, whereas the man may not have intended to be threatening. If there is no universal standard of behaviour then the 'reasonable person' test is impossible to apply. Whose judgment should apply?

Feminist legal theorists, like critical legal theorists, have also pointed out that, irrespective of the label of a test, it is the judge's views that will prevail. This raises a different practical problem about the way in which judges are appointed. Given that there are so few women judges then it is likely that a male view of what is 'reasonable' will prevail.

FREEDOM

Feminist legal theorists have often been more concerned to discuss the problem of how to define 'equality' (and the problem of the equality/difference debate) than to think about freedom. However, there are some recent, interesting analyses of freedom from a feminist perspective. Feminists have focused on the practical constraints on women's lives, for example, under which circumstances are women able to leave violent men? The law tends to look at individuals outside of their social context and therefore assumes that someone makes a choice out of their own individual 'free will'. Feminist legal theory, in common with critical legal theory, highlights the importance of the social context within which decisions are made. For example, a battered woman may decide to stay because she has children and is economically dependent upon a man. Were she given better options and more support, she would be able to move to safety with her children. Whilst many philosophical arguments on free will are abstract, feminist legal theory tends to draw from concrete examples of problems arising in an unequal society as the starting point for their theoretical analyses.

It is generally accepted that feminism promotes freedom for women, irrespective of the choices they make. The concern is that they may find it difficult to challenge certain assumptions. The consciousness-raising movement in the 1960s was based upon the idea that the existing norms of behaviour in society were so pervasive and difficult to challenge that women accepted a degree of subordination without questioning it. This raises questions about the extent to which our choices can be viewed as 'free'. In 'consciousness-raising' meetings women could informally compare their experiences with other women. This was particularly important because some women had been beaten up at home (or were sexually harassed at work) but felt either that it was their fault or that such behaviour had to be put up with as part of women's lot; shame could also prevent them from talking about it. If you compare your experiences with those of others, it is possible to discover that you are exposed to similar problems that arise from social attitudes which, for example, routinely treat women as available sex objects for men.

The 1960s also saw the rise of other social movements such as struggles against racism and homophobia. Black women and gay women made it clear that the feminist movement should represent all women and not simply be a tool of white middle class women who wanted greater freedom to access the professions.

RELATIONSHIP BETWEEN FEMINIST LEGAL THEORY AND PRACTICE IN LAW

Recently there have been a number of debates in the journal *Feminist Legal Studies* about the relationship between feminist legal theory and feminist legal practice. Feminist legal practice includes the work of solicitors and barristers who are concerned with practising law in a way that changes the law and so has a practical impact upon women's lives. Importantly, as the Norwegian legal feminist Tove Dahl has pointed out, this need not be about issues that are necessarily classed as 'women's issues' such as discrimination law; welfare law affects more women than discrimination law for example. Her argument was that, when it comes to law reform, feminists should concentrate on trying to improve the laws that actually affect women in practice.

Feminist legal theory is not simply concerned with improving the law. Its reach is broader in terms of the subjects analysed, and jurisprudence and philosophy are drawn upon to problematise theoretical issues arising out of the relationship between women and law (e.g. what do terms like 'freedom' and 'equality' mean?). Feminist legal theory is also critical of the ways in which legal and political philosophers have made sexist assumptions about women and so it considers how (and whether) this has affected their work. Often the position of women is revealed to be a 'blind spot' for traditional writers. By focusing upon the view of women in these theorists' work, feminist legal theorists have elicited weaknesses and contradictions in their arguments. Far from being merely critical, there is often an additional creative aspect to this engagement: feminist legal theorists then say how they would improve the theory to make it applicable to women, as well as to men. For two of many examples, see Susan Moller Okin's reading of John Rawls in SM Okin, *Justice, Gender and the Family* (New York: Basic Books, 1991) or Carole Pateman's analysis of Thomas Hobbes in C Pateman, *The Sexual Contract* (Cambridge: Polity Press, 1988). Whilst this can lead to some abstract debates in feminist legal theory, the key concern remains that women's practical position be improved.

RELATIONSHIP BETWEEN FEMINIST LEGAL THEORY AND POLITICAL PHILOSOPHY

There are areas of overlap between different areas of political philosophy and feminist legal theory. For example, there are liberal, socialist, Marxist and anarchist feminists who have different views about law. Liberal feminists accept the main liberal ideals, such as the view that the State should not impose any idea of what is good upon anyone; that citizens should have rights to live their life in their own way, providing that others are not harmed. However, they need to extend the 'harm principle' to include harm to women that occurs within the home. Liberal feminists support 'formal equality': basically, the view that men and women should be treated in the same way and have equality of opportunity. This can be contrasted with 'substantive equality', which refers to equality of outcome, which may involve giving additional help to someone who starts with a disadvantage.

In contrast to liberal feminists, socialist feminists believe that part of the problem for women in our society is that they live in a capitalist society in which workers (as well as women) are exploited. Socialist feminists want to see a change in the workplace as well as in the treatment of women. This involves an emphasis upon employment protection laws that have been won by trade unions, a preference for State-run over private-run enterprise, the welfare state and further protective measures against exploitation generally.

Similarly, Marxist feminists draw upon the work of Karl Marx to argue that workers are exploited because they have no choice but to work for 'capitalists', i.e. those people who own the means of production. They are forced to sell their ability to work as if it were a commodity. This means not only that they are exploited economically by being underpaid, but also that they do not have control over the way in which they work and lack the fulfilment that Marx thought that work should provide. This is still the case for women who are still engaged in more menial jobs than men, over which they have little control. For Marxist feminists, the main solution to subordination (of both female and male workers) is the communal ownership of the means of production. This is no longer a particularly popular position, although that in itself is not an argument against it.

Anarchist feminists are also a rare group who believe that the State is part of the problem for women and hence do not believe in law. Most feminist legal theorists recognise that changes in law may not solve women's problems, which derive from social attitudes to women, but think that law can be used as an instrument to try to change attitudes, for example, by the use of the Sex Discrimination Act 1975, the Equal Pay Act 1970.

More broadly, feminists have challenged the meaning of the term 'political'. Some contemporary continental philosophy – some of which has been broadly termed 'postmodernism' or 'post-structuralism' – has been influential in feminist legal theory. This has included asking the question: how is the meaning of 'woman' defined by our use of language? These feminist legal theorists have pointed to problems involving 'essentialism' (i.e. the view that women have some fixed underlying defining characteristic in common). They stress both that the meaning of what it is to be a woman changes in different societies and the relationship between language and power.

QUEER THEORY

More recently, feminist thinkers have gone beyond challenging the naturalness of gender roles and associated cultural expectations. The very anatomical bipartition of human beings into either men or women is now in question. The belief in a biological complementarity between the sexes has been termed *heteronormativity* by Judith Butler, an extremely influential philosopher in queer theory and feminist legal studies. Butler's critique of heteronormativity in *Gender Trouble* (1991) is based on the idea of *gender performativity*. Language produces reality, including anatomical reality – it is not because there are two different types of sexual organs that there are only two sexes. Butler argues that there are as many genders as there are people. This is why the term 'queer theory' is slowly gaining ground over Gay/Lesbian theory. Queer theory does not merely claim equal rights for women or for homosexuals but goes further. It contests the very idea of fixed gendered or sexual identities. Queer essentially means 'not normative' and rests on the idea that identities consist of so many components that to define a person through a single characteristic is not descriptive but performative, and thus normative and violent. Basically, queer theory challenges sexual difference as the main structuring principle of all human societies thus far.

The legal consequences of challenging heteronormativity are momentous, especially for family law. Not only does it challenge the heterosexual, nuclear family as the natural, biological model by arguing that the biological model is itself constructed through language, acts and rituals, but it also challenges the idea that a child should only have two parents. Today, English law recognises the same adoption (Adoption and Children Act 2002, Civil Partnership Act 2004) and IVF rights (Human Fertilisation and Embryology Act 2008) to heterosexual and homosexual couples. Heteronormativity is slowly receding as the governing principle both of sexual and parental relations. And recent cases have recognised parental rights over the same child to more than two parents. Thus in *Re D (Contact and PR: Lesbian mothers and known father)* [2006] a sperm donor was granted rights as a third parent in addition to the lesbian couple,

You should now be confident that you would be able to tick all the boxes on the checklist at the beginning of this chapter. To check your knowledge of Feminist legal theory why not visit the companion website and take the Multiple Choice Question test. Check your understanding of the terms and vocabulary used in this chapter with the flashcard glossary.

9

Critical legal studies

ORIGINS AND AIMS OF CRITICAL LEGAL STUDIES

WHAT ARE CRITICAL LEGAL STUDIES?

In the narrow sense, the term Critical Legal Studies refers to a movement which originated in the US in the 1970s as a response to an increasing political and legal conservatism. It can be traced back to American Legal Realism, especially insofar as it emphasises the plurality of perspectives on law, but is a distinct movement emerging in the 1970s. This movement is, for all intents and purposes, now defunct. The name, however, endures: in the broad sense, Critical Legal Studies, or CLS, encompass a plurality of different critical perspectives on law which have been flourishing for the past three decades. As the abbreviation CLS is often used to refer to the movement, so is the term 'crit' used to refer to its participants.

It is impossible to define the CLS movement in a definitive manner as CLS perspectives are ever expanding. They range from analysing legal symbolism and representations of law in literature to deconstructing the concepts of legal discourse and questioning the symptomatology of the law (is the law neutral, as it claims to be, or is it patriarchal, discriminatory, colonial, exclusionary, driven by anxiety etc?).

Yet all CLS perspectives share a wish to critique the traditional notions of legal objectivity and supposed neutrality of the law in order to reveal law as a murkier, much more morally ambivalent area than is usually acknowledged in classic legal discourse. The law can be shown, for example, to manipulate legal concepts in order retroactively to legitimate the expropriation of indigenous people, or to entrench racial or sexual stereotypes.

What, however, distinguishes CLS from more straightforwardly critical takes on law is that its many approaches import insights, concepts and methods devised by other disciplines such as aesthetics, literary criticism, psychoanalysis and philosophy into the critical study of the law.

- The shared idea is that there is another 'truth' to law than that of its apparent content, though the status of this other truth – hidden, repressed, absent, impossible, ambivalent – depends on the views of the author.

- The CLS movement was officially born in the US in 1977 at a conference at the University of Wisconsin-Madison, but its founding members were rooted in 1960s' activism, particularly the civil rights movement and anti-Vietnam War militantism.

- CLS proponents imported the ideas, theories, and philosophies of predominantly European thinkers (initially Marx and the Frankfurt School) into the field of law, thereby giving birth to the idea of a critical inquiry into what had hitherto been constructed as an objective, quasi-scientific field of study.

- The central object of CLS, if one is to be named, is to challenge the apparent objectivity of law and legal practice in order to expose the political choices embedded in legal discourse.

- The forms adopted by this challenge are many, depending essentially on which theory is being applied: CLS range from the straightforward, neo-Marxist denunciation of the function of the law in the reproduction and legitimation of the social *status quo* to the deconstruction of a legal concept (after Derrida) or the exposure of the repressed content of the law (after Freud).

The CLS movement includes several other movements: feminist legal theory, queer theory, critical race theory, postcolonial theory. It retains critical inquiry into the nature and functioning of law as its federating feature.

AMERICAN CLS

THE EMERGENCE OF CLS

In the US, classical jurisprudence, informed by a belief in and devotion to the grandeur of the law, dominated law schools until the 1970s, with the liberal influence of the Warren Supreme Court acting as a punctual corrector of the conservatism of legal academics. In 1970 Duncan Kennedy, a student at Yale Law School, started expressing strong dissatisfaction with the smugness of legal academics, safely sheltered behind the 'objectivity' of the formal rule of law. Put otherwise, Duncan Kennedy questioned the apparent absence of politics from the legal discourse. Clearly, in the US the beginning of the crit movement was informed by a general distrust of authority fuelled by the Vietnam War, and so of the law.

The central claim of the early American crits was that the grand legal edifice, despite its self-representation as neutral, objective and abstract, was in fact deeply *political*, structurally *contingent*, fundamentally *contradictory* and *indeterminate* (the idea that law does not determine the outcome of legal disputes but politics do), and that the law's main function was to entrench the social *status quo* further by conferring legitimacy upon it (*legitimation*). It is in this sense that the early crit movement was influenced by Marx's view of the world in terms of domination, exploitation and oppression.

The initial object of American CLS, particularly that of Duncan Kennedy, was twofold:

■ to 'counteract the conservatizing effect of legal training' in legal education;

■ to turn the law into an overt political terrain.

Prominent participants in the American CLS movement include Duncan Kennedy, Mark Tushnet and Roberto Unger.

THE DECLINE OF FIRST-GENERATION AMERICAN CLS

The early American crit movement came to a premature halt, partly due to the opposition of mainstream legal academics who feared for their own position (effectively, crits were not hired by law schools and so the movement stopped developing) and partly due to the movement's own conceptual shortcomings: the concepts of *legitimation, contradiction* and *indeterminacy* proposed by the early crits became the site of theoretical debates with the mainstream legal academy, which was unfortunate as these concepts referred to oppositional strategies and so were not theoretical building blocks for the creation of an alternative legal discourse. These debates resulted in the explosive potential of the concepts of early CLS being defused through appropriation by mainstream legal thought. Thus for example:

■ The concepts of *contradiction* and *indeterminacy* led to *neo-pragmatism*: since the law is indeterminate and contradictory let us be practical about it and abandon grand theories.

■ *Legitimation*: if everything is political then let us be aware of it and make the politics explicit. This led to the 'reason-giving', 'civic-republican', 'dialogic' strand of mainstream legal thought (cf P Schlag).

AMERICAN CLS TODAY

Though the American CLS movement in its original form more or less ended in the 1980s as a radical challenge to mainstream legal thought, its legacy in the US is alive and well as feminist legal theory (fem-crit) and race critical theory (race-crit).

There is also a more general movement, heir to first-generation American CLS and represented in the Association for the Study of Law, Culture, and the Humanities. The ASLCH, which holds annual conferences in the US, is an association committed to interdisciplinary legal scholarship: legal history, legal theory and jurisprudence, law and cultural studies, law and literature, law and the performing arts, and legal hermeneutics are all represented. The Association's remit is to contextualise – and so problematise – law by exploring its relation with culture, politics and society. For example, in *Law in the Liberal Arts* (2004) Austin Sarat argues that the traditional location of legal education in law schools offering vocational training produces an impoverishment of students' – and so lawyers' – grasp of the law's place in culture and society.

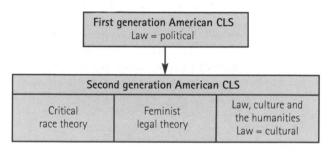

ENGLISH CLS

Much as in the US, Marx was the immediate background to CLS in the UK until the early 1980s. At that time:

■ the rise of individualism and its corollary, the decline of faith in collectivism, led to a weakening of the Marxist framework's influence;

■ theoretical challenges to the Marxist concepts of ideology, historical materialism and so on led to a dissatisfaction with the conceptual tools introduced by the German political economist a century previously.

The disaffection with a thought structured in terms of historical forces and material conditions led Britcrits to turn to a number of theories in which the subject – or its problematisation – was, in one way or another, central: the new influences of Britcrits were to be psychoanalysis (Freud and Lacan), genealogy (Nietzsche, Foucault) and post-structuralism (Derrida).

PSYCHOANALYSIS

Sigmund Freud (1856–1939)

Freud, who 'discovered' the unconscious in the late 19th century by noticing that physical symptoms had psychical significations and so could be lifted through the 'talking cure', was the inventor of the psychoanalytic technique. One of Freud's early examples is that of a patient who suffers from hydrophobia and recalls, during the treatment, having been disgusted when she saw a dog drink out of a cup at a time of great personal stress.

Most of Freud's work is an elaboration of clinical concepts designed to alleviate psychical suffering without trying to get people to consciously improve. The idea is, instead, to tap into the unknown causes of their behaviour. However, a significant portion of his work also develops the clinical insights of psycho-analysis in order to elucidate a number of puzzling, and recurrent, phenomena of civilisation such as religious guilt, love of authority and so on (essentially *Totem and Taboo, Moses and Monotheism, Group Psychology* and *Civilisation and its Discontents*). In these works Freud's central thesis is that religion is indi-vidual neuroses brought to the power of 'a neurosis of humanity'. Freud started with the observation that similar affects can be found in the unconscious and in the religious scriptures of the Judaeo-Christian tradition:

- love for figures of authority;

- certain prohibitions (*a minima*, incest and parricide);

- a sense of culpability concerning prohibited desires;

- the possibility of redemption through renunciation of these desires.

In order to account for the parallelism between religion and the unconscious, Freud posits, *ex post facto*, the universal – and mythical – origin of civilisation, and so of the unconscious.

The origin of law

In *Totem and Taboo* the story unfolds as follows: in ancient times a man, known as the 'father of the primal horde', kept all the women of the tribe to himself and so expelled all his male descendants. One day the sons grew sick of the situation and united to kill and then eat the father to appropriate his potency. Belatedly seized by remorse, they erected a totem to the father (henceforth symbolising the empty place of the lawgiver) and instituted the incest prohibition so that they would not benefit from their crime by enjoying the women of the tribe. This prefigures the social contract: the sons agreed to leave the place of power empty and so to be *equal before the law*. From that point on, repression (of desire), guilt (with regard to the original sin), love of authority (the totem) and law-abiding as redemptive pathway, the structuring parameters of the neurotic unconscious in Freudian times, all find themselves accounted for through a myth which also functions as that of the origin of the law (in his later work *Moses and Monotheism* Freud retraces these structural elements through the scriptures of the Judaeo-Christian religions).

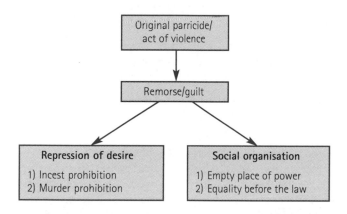

So for Freud, civilisation originates in violence, which gives rise to guilt. In order to alleviate this guilt and to avoid the repetition of such violence, individuals unite and decide to lay strict guidelines for the social organisation of desire on the one hand and to empty the place of power on the other, so that all are equal before the law (again, to avoid anger and so further violence). The Freudian myth has been used by postcolonial theory to argue that violence against indigenous peoples is the violent, repressed origin of colonial legal systems.

Freud concludes that the discourses of civilisation, and primarily of law, function as the *superego of culture* (i.e. the law tells you not to give in to impulses such as killing anyone who annoys you, or sleeping with whomever you fancy). Building on this hypothesis, a number of thinkers have argued that law, the superego of culture, represses the singular desires of its subjects and that these repressed desires can be revealed using the method devised by Freud to uncover the repressed content of the unconscious.

Jacques Lacan (1901–81)

French psychiatrist Jacques Lacan initiated a return to Freud in the early 1950s that incorporated the many influences he had been exposed to in his formative years: Hegelian and Heideggerian philosophy, Merleau-Ponty's phenomenology, Saussurian linguistics, structural anthropology etc. Out of the mythical psycho-analysis invented by Freud, Lacan created a (post)structuralist form of psycho-analysis in which 'the unconscious is structured like a language' and the incest prohibition is merely a contingent, cultural rendition of the natural impossibility for man to exist without law. In Lacan's early work in particular:

- ■ law, or the symbolic order, is not what deprives the subject of the truth of his desire but, on the contrary, is a necessity for the subject, who needs the support of symbolic networks in order to structure its psychical reality;

- ■ the Oedipus complex is merely one of the ways in which the invariant struc-ture of the subject, uncovered by Freud as marked by an empty place and a prohibition, can be accounted for.

One of the key insights of Lacanian psychoanalysis for CLS is the convincing argument that psychical reality is always framed by the subject's own fantasy: in other words there is no such thing as reality, there are only fantasmatic realities constructed through subjective interpretative processes. As such for Lacan, though action is of course vital, true resistance starts with the subject resisting their own interpretative process in order to be able to separate themselves from their fantasy. The difficulty of applying Lacan's insights to law is self-evident: most of the work of resistance should take place in analysis and it is only subsequently that resistance can be displaced onto the political scene.

CLS applications of psychoanalysis

Psychoanalytic inquiry into the possibility of deciphering the repressed content of the law with the help of the Freudian theory of the superego was developed by French legal academic Pierre Legendre and in the UK by Peter Goodrich. The key idea is that legal subjects come to love authority figures through a complex mechanism of displacement: I give up some of my sexual desires by abiding by certain laws; this repressed libidinal energy is then desexualised and displaced onto authority figures. This is why we accept and even enjoy the law.

As to Lacan, in his numerous works, Slovenian philosopher Slavoj Žižek borrows many concepts from Lacanian psychoanalysis to interpret political events, introducing, for instance, the concepts of fantasy and enjoyment in the realm of politics. For example in *Tarrying with the Negative* (1993), Žižek presents a psychoanalytically informed account of racism in terms of what is perceived as the other's theft of the national enjoyment. Thus a common racist complaint is that 'immigrants steal our women and our work'. Žižek interprets this as a version of the frequent fantasy that the other is always having more fun than I am and so steals my enjoyment

GENEALOGY

Michel Foucault (1926–84)
Another extremely important thought for CLS is that of Michel Foucault, who devised the genealogical method. This method is a mixture of history and philosophy applied to the human sciences.

The subject
After studying at the *Ecole Normale Supérieure* in Paris, Foucault dedicated his life and work to opposing the two main currents of thought that prevailed at the time: Marxist thought and phenomenology. Foucault's critique focused on conceptions of the subject:

■ for Marxism the subject is objectively constituted by his material conditions;

■ for phenomenology the subject is an empty, a-historical locus cognising the present.

Starting with this double rejection of the thought of his time, Foucault set out to demonstrate that the subject was neither the mere product of its conditions nor an abstract, eternal transcendence freely cognising real phenomena.

Foucault's own view is that the 'subject' does not exist as a closed entity but that it would be more accurate to speak of the forms of subjectivity which are attendant to modes of discourse.

To give a simple example: in the 19th century psychology was invented as a science of man: man became an object of knowledge for man. Psychology is a *discourse*, which comes with certain *practices* such as psychometric testing, and the psychologist, i.e. the one that speaks the discourse of psychology and carries out the psychometric tests, operates with a *form of subjectivity* that is attendant to psychology as discourse and its practices. Put simply, the psychologist constructs his reality (or the way he understands the world) in the terms of the discourse he uses professionally. So the psychologist is neither simply the product of the world into which he is born (for he plays a part in implementing, interpreting, expanding, developing the discourse within which he operates) nor an a-historical subject standing outside of discourse (for his very mode of apprehending phenomena, other beings, is structured by the categories of his discourse so that it is no longer possible for him to see things otherwise than in the terms of his discourse).

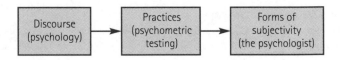

For Foucault the appropriate field of inquiry is constituted by all three domains taken together. You cannot just study a discourse, or practices, as if they were objective. You also have to interrogate the forms of subjectivity attendant to a discipline.

Genealogies
Starting from this very strong epistemological claim, Foucault proceeds to write histories, which he calls genealogies, of certain discourse (e.g. human sciences: *The Archaeology of Knowledge*), institutions (e.g. the prison in *Discipline and Punish*) and practices (e.g. confession, psychoanalysis in *The Will to Knowledge*).

■ Foucault carries out philosophically inspired histories of the human sciences (medicine, psychology and criminology are singled out as sciences that take man as object of knowledge).

■ One of Foucault's key inspirations is Nietzschean philosophy, which expresses dissatisfaction with the idea of truth as absolute.

■ For Foucault, 'truth' is always contingent, constructed, made to look objective and so 'true'.

■ The point is to show how something that appears to be absolutely true and so unquestionable ('all criminals should go to prison' and 'all madmen to asylums') is in fact recent and contingent. For example imprisonment as punishment only began in the 19th century and yet it is seen as the only way to deal with crime.

■ In order to show that what appears to be true is in fact historically constructed, Foucault writes genealogies: historical analyses of the micro-processes of power that eventually produced what appears as truth today.

■ Hence, Foucault's work aims to produce histories of the present: how did the present come about? For example, why is the prison so important today when it had never been in the history of mankind?

Genealogies and politics

A corollary of Foucault's momentous challenge of objectivity of discourse is the exposure of the voluntary subjection of people to the discourses and practices of power. The political purpose of Foucault's genealogies, if there were to be one, would be to open a space for non-naive forms of resistances, i.e. forms of resistances that take account of the degree to which those that resist are part of the discourse that they oppose. According to Foucault, failure to do so only makes power stronger.

For example, if a law is in place but never implemented, and as a form of resistance you transgress that law, then the law is applied, legal precedents are produced, and the law you thought you were resisting is now stronger than before your transgression.

Foucault's method, which is to concentrate on micro-processes of power (for example, the minute details of prison/factory life) rather than on grand analyses of power as a whole, has been taken up in the US and the UK in governmentality studies, social studies, social control theory and risk theory.

POST-STRUCTURALISM AND DECONSTRUCTION

Lastly, post-structuralism, and particularly the deconstructive method, have exerted significant influence on CLS over the past 20 years.

■ Post-structuralism names a series of rejections of structuralism because of the distaste associated with thinking that there are structures governing our minds and thought processes.

■ Deconstruction, a reading method pioneered by French philosopher Jacques Derrida, seeks to reveal the hidden, repressed or unconscious contents of an author's writing.

■ The deconstructive method is that of a close reading; it works by re-introducing the plurality of meanings of a key term to show that what appears to be a simple, descriptive statement or application of a law in fact conceals certain political choices made by the author.

■ If it is possible to do so, post-structuralist thinkers argue, it is because language is by definition incomplete. In other words, for a text to make sense we need to refer to a *supplement*: the context of the text, the person of the author, the context of the reader.

STRUCTURALISM AND POST-STRUCTURALISM

Post-structuralism is so called because it came about as a critique of the structuralist movement. The structuralist movement started with Ferdinand de Saussure's structural linguistics and was developed essentially by anthropologist Claude Lévi-Strauss and then by Roland Barthes as a method of literary criticism. Foucault and Lacan are also sometimes associated with the structuralist movement though they both rapidly moved away from structuralism, having nonetheless taken account of the importance of structures and language: this allowed them to move beyond the classical notion of the subject as *agency, intentionality* and *unity of consciousness*.

The main idea of structuralism is that the elements of a given structure only make sense in relation to each other. So for Saussure the linguist a word or signifier only makes sense in relation to other words; for Lévi-Strauss the anthropologist the rituals and symbols of a tribe only make sense when taken in relation to one another; and for Barthes the same logic applies to the reading of a novel or poem. Structuralists themselves were quick to see that if the elements of a structure only made sense in relation to each other then there lacked a point of fixed sense from which to initiate the process of interconnected meaning-making, and soon enough theoretical devices or *supplements*, as Derrida would later call them, such as the floating signifier (Lévi-Strauss) or *potlatch* (Marcel Mauss), were introduced to remedy the impasse of structuralist theory.

POST-STRUCTURALISM

The key idea of post-structuralist thought is that it is impossible by definition to represent the whole of 'reality' in language – this is why it criticises the *metaphysics of presence*, or, put simply, the idea that we could represent ourselves to ourselves accurately and exhaustively in language, an idea that had organised Western philosophy since Plato. So when we read a text or hear a speech there is always something *in excess* of what is being said and this is what gives sense to the text/speech: this is the *supplement* which the structuralists had been looking for.

DECONSTRUCTION AND CLS

A basic application of the method of deconstruction could take the form of revealing that a given legal term, with an apparently neutral and unambiguous meaning, in fact conceals a number of other meanings that are hidden or repressed and yet nonetheless inhabit a given decision. The deconstruction of a legal concept aims to reveal the latent ambivalence of a decision of law.

For example, the criminal defence of insanity (or M'Naghten Rules): some clinically insane criminals stand trial and serve a full sentence because their insanity does not preclude them from being aware that what they are doing is wrong. That is because the apparently neutral concept of insanity at law in fact already contains the implicit decision to punish the insane in the same way as the sane provided there is an awareness of wrongdoing. In this sense, perverts and psychopaths who know that what they are doing is wrong are considered to be sane for the purposes of the law, though they may well end up serving their sentences in hospitals such as Broadmoor. By revealing the hidden plurality of meanings ascribable to the notion of insanity the deconstructive work will shatter the fiction of the law's neutrality.

THE PHILOSOPHICAL BEYOND OF DECONSTRUCTION

Beyond the relatively simple deconstruction of instantiated legal concepts (i.e. legal terms employed by the courts), some of the work carried out by crits has more philosophical ambition. For example, the relation of law to justice, sovereignty and violence is the subject of a very important text delivered by Derrida in the US in 1989, entitled 'Force of Law: "The Mystical Foundation of Authority" ' (*Cardozo Law Review* 11: 1990). In this text, Derrida draws on his work on language to deconstruct law – or rather, to argue that if law is always deconstructible it is because justice lies beyond it: and so deconstruction takes place *in the name of justice*. Justice is infinite, whereas law is finite: in other words, the legal response made to the Other who is before the law (the legal subject) ineluctably falls short of justice, which is an *infinite going out to the other* and so impossible. Indeed, since every subject is *singular*, and since law is *universal*, it follows that law cannot do justice to singularity. Because justice is impossible, this impossibility remains lodged at the heart of the legal decision. It haunts it and so deconstructs the law from within: for the law operates according to a logic of calculation, and not out of infinite responsiveness to singularity. Though classically we see law as just for treating everyone in the same way, for Derrida law always falls short of justice *for the same reason*. This does not mean we should not have law, but that law should not be mistaken for justice.

You should now be confident that you would be able to tick all the boxes on the checklist at the beginning of this chapter. To check your knowledge of Critical legal studies why not visit the companion website and take the Multiple Choice Question test. Check your understanding of the terms and vocabulary used in this chapter with the flashcard glossary.

10

Putting it into practice...

Now that you've mastered the basics, you will want to put it all into practice. The Routledge Questions and Answers series provides an ideal opportunity for you to apply your understanding and knowledge of the law and to hone your essay-writing technique.

We've included one exam-style essay question, which replicates the type of question posed in the Routledge Questions and Answers series to give you some essential exam practice. The Q&A includes an answer plan and a fully worked model answer to help you recognise what examiners might look for in your answer.

QUESTION 1

How does an insight into the 'viewpoint' of a legal theorist concerning law help in understanding the work of the legal theorist?

ANSWER PLAN

The question concerns the general question of the role that a legal theorist's viewpoint has on the understanding of the legal theorist's theory of law. The answer identifies three general viewpoints that a legal theorist might take on the institution we call 'law':

(1) The lawyers or participant's perspective where the legal theorist seeks to explain law in terms of a lawyers understanding of law. Dworkin and Kelsen are the beast known examples of this perspective.

(2) The institutional 'engaged' perspective where the legal theorist goes beyond the lawyers perspective and examines law in its wider political and social perspective but this perspective has some strong commitment to a particular type of legal system or an ideal form of law. Finnis, Galligan and MacCormick are all strong examples of this type of approach.

(3) The 'detached' institutional perspective where the legal theorist examines law in its social and political context – the 'institutional setting of law' – but has no express commitment to law or legal systems of any kind. This value-free descriptive jurisprudence is best exemplified by Professor Hart.

A skeleton plan is suggested.

- Introduction

- the importance of identifying a legal theorist's perspective on law

- ▓ three different types of perspectives on law: the lawyer's perspective, the institutional 'engaged' and the institutional 'detached'

- ▓ discussion of the legal theory perspectives of Dworkin, Kelsen, Finnis, Galligan, MacCormick, Hart

- ▓ conclusion: understanding perspectives on legal theory vital to understanding legal theory.

Jurisprudence can seem bewildering to the new student as a mass of theorists and theories are suddenly upon the student who is expected to absorb, digest and feedback a body of knowledge that seems part philosophy, part sociology, part history but bearing little relation in content to traditional law subjects.

One way of imposing order over the chaos is to try to obtain a sense of where a particular legal theorist stands in relation to the law. Understanding the standpoint of a legal theorist makes understanding that legal theorist easier as well as permitting the construction of a 'mind map' so that important jurisprudential scholars can be fitted into that 'mind map' schemata.

It is suggested that three broad standpoints could be identified in order to place a range of authors in a 'viewpoint mind map'. These authors include: Dworkin, Kelsen, Galligan, MacCormick, Finnis, Austin, Bentham, Hart and Raz.

The three viewpoints or standpoint perspectives are:

(1) Participant perspectives – Dworkin, Kelsen.
(2) Institutional (or 'external') engaged perspective – MacCormick, Galligan, Finnis.
(3) Institutional (or 'external') detached perspective – Hart, Austin.

The participant perspective can also be termed the 'lawyers perspective'. This perspective seeks to give an account of the social institution we call law from the point of view of the court-room or a judge. To a certain extent this perspective is a 'natural' one for a legal theorist to take. As Profeesor Raz comments in 'The Nature of Law' in *Ethics in the Public Domain* (1994):

> 'most theorists tend to be by education and profession lawyers, and their audience often consists primarily of law students. Quite naturally and imperceptibly they adopted the lawyer's perspective on the law.'

The problem with the participant or lawyers perspective on the law is that it can lead the legal theorist who adopts it to neglect important features of law because the lawyers perspective fails to examine law in the wider political context in which the law is moored. Two legal theorists who adopted the lawyers perspective are Hans Kelsen and Ronald Dworkin.

With regard to Kelsen he took explaining the 'normativity' or authority of the law as the backbone of his theory of law. This in itself is a question which looks at law from the lawyers perspective – what sense Kelsen asked to give to claims of 'ought' in the law? As Kelsen comments in 'Introduction to the Problems of Legal Theory' (1934):

> 'The Pure Theory of Law works with this basic norm as a hypothetical foundation. Given this presupposition that the basic norm is valid, the legal system resting on it is also valid. . . . Rooted in the basic norm, ultimately, is the normative import of all the material facts constituting the legal system. The empirical data given to legal interpretation can be interpreted as law, that is, as a system of basic norms, only if a basic norm is presupposed.'

Therefore for Kelsen, a person who regards a legal order as valid as opposed to a mere coercive order presupposes a hypothetical 'basic norm' which gives 'normativity' or 'oughtness' to the legal system so interpreted as valid. Kelsen is seeking to explain what lawyers mean when they say 'the law says you ought not to do X or you ought to do X'. The persepective of Kelsen is the lawyers perspective, trying to give sense to 'lawyers talk' of legal obligation. As Kelsen comments in 'Pure Theory of Law' (1967) 'the decisive question' is why the demands of a legal organ are considered valid but not the demands of a gang of robbers. The answer to this question is that only the demands of a legal organ are interpreted as an objectively valid norm because the person viewing the legal order as valid and therefore more than a coercive order, more than a 'gang of robbers', is presupposing in his own consciousness a basic norm which gives validity, normative force to the legal order.

Kelsen's basic question in legal theory – what sense to give to lawyers statements of 'legal ought' – is a question from the lawyers perspective, but this tendency to examine the law from the lawyer's or participant's perspective, is reinforced by Kelsen's methodology. Kelsen insisted that his theory was a 'pure theory of law'. He regarded it as doubly pure. It is pure of all moral argument and it is pure of all sociological facts. The view of law examined by Kelsen is free of any kind of moral evaluation such as what moral purposes the law could serve or sociological enquiry as for example what motivates persons to obey the law. Kelsen merely looks at the raw data of legal experience to be found in the statute books and law reports and asks: what sense to give to legal talk of 'ought'?

For a legal theory to ignore the moral and sociological realities framing the law it must be the case that that legal theory is focusing purely on the lawyer's perspective. Although Kelsen has an interesting and developed theory answering the lawyer's question of what sense to give to lawyer's talk of legal obligation, legal duty and legal 'ought', Kelsen's theory of law has little general explanatory power of the social institution called law. Moreover by clinging so exclusively to the 'lawyer's perspective' Kelsen makes statements that from a wider perspective seem unjustifiable. For example Kelsen comments in 'Introduction to the Problems of Legal Theory' (1934):

> 'the law is a coercive apparatus having in and of itself no political or ethical value'.

Kelsen should have considered that the law can have value in itself as a means by which citizens can express loyalty and identification with their community. The law as an expression of a particular community can be the focus of a citizen's loyalty as a form of self-identification with a particular community. This point – recognised by modern writers on law such as Raz and Leslie Green – would have been lost on Kelsen, buried as he was in the lawyer's perspective.

Kelsen's theory of law was once termed by the political thinker Harold Laski as 'an exercise in logic not in life' (see H. Laski 'A Grammar of Politics' 1938). We may interpret this statement by Laski as meaning that although Kelsen tries impressively to answer the question concerning the law's normativity, Kelsen has little of value to say about law as a social phenomenon generally.

The lawyer's or participant viewpoint on law can be valuable but it is unreasonable to study the law solely and exclusively from the lawyer's perspective. The law must be examined, in order to get full explanatory power of this important social institution, in the wider perspective of social organizations and political institutions generally. This wider perspective may be termed the 'institutional' or 'external' perspective on law and has been the dominant viewpoint in at least English jurisprudence from Thomas Hobbes in the seventeenth century to Professor Hart.

However before we examine the 'institutional' perspective on law we need to examine another famous example of the lawyer's perspective, that of Professor Ronald Dworkin's theory of law.

Dworkin's preoccupation with his theory of law has been to answer the question: how can law be so interpreted so as to provide a sound justification for the use of State coercion involved in forcing the payment of compensation in a civil action at law? This is again a lawyer's question although a different lawyer's question from Kelsen's preoccupation with the normativity of the law. Dworkin's theory of law is aimed at the justification of State coercion expressed through law. Dworkin has taken appellate case decisions as his testing ground for his theory of law which has involved the controversial proposition that the law of the Anglo-American legal system involves not just the accepted case law and statutes but also includes the best moral interpretation of that law. Therefore there is a greater connection between Dworkin's lawyer's perspective and general legal theory than Kelsen's lawyers perspective which seemed grounded on the normativity of law only. Dworkin's theory of law at least engages with the debate 'what is law?' or 'what are the grounds of law?' However despite Dworkin's connection to wider debates in legal theory about the nature of law Dworkin seeks to answer that question from the lawyer's perspective. Dworkin has defended his pre-occupation with the courtroom by observing that it is the courtroom that the doctrinal question of 'what is law?' is most acutely answered. Dworkin comments in 'Hart and the Concepts of Law' (2006) Harvard Law Review Forum:

> 'Courtrooms symbolise the practical importance of the doctrinal question and I have often used both judicial decisions both as empirical data and illustrations for my doctrinal claims.'

Dworkin has often used appellate cases to support his arguments leading to the charge that he is developing a legal theory out of a theory of adjudication. Dworkin uses the House of Lords appellate case of *McLouglinh v O'Brien* [1982] as the centre piece for testing of various theories of law including his own theory known as 'Law as Integrity' at pp 230–240 of *Law's Empire*, Dworkin's magnum opus on legal theory from 1986. The United States appellate court decisions of the Supreme Court have been use by Dworkin, namely: the 'snail darter' case *Tennessee Valley Authority v Hill* [1978] and *Brown v U.S.* [1954] – both discussed by Dworkin in *Law's Empire* at pp 20–23 and pp 29–30 respectively. A case used by Dworkin in the 1960s to illustrate his arguments about the nature of law, 'Elmer's case' is used again at pp 15–20 of *Law's Empire*. 'Elmer's case' is known properly as *Riggs v Palmer* [1883], an appellate decision of the New York appeals court.

Due to Dworkin's lawyer's perspective on the law, his tendency to look at the law through the prism of the courtroom has led to criticism that Dworkin has developed a theory of law out of a theory of adjudication. As Professor Raz argues in 'Between Authority and Interpretation' (2009) of Dworkin's *Law's Empire*:

> 'His book is not much an explanation of the law as a sustained argument about how courts, especially American and British courts should decide cases. It contains a theory of adjudication rather than a theory of the nature of law.'

The argument against Dworkin is that his obsession with the courtroom, the lawyer's perspective on law, is that Dworkin can miss or fail to appreciate essential features of law as law operates in the wider social context beyond the courtroom. For example Dworkin fails in his legal theory to account for the law's claim to authority, which is an important part of the law's method of social organization. Dworkin says a lot about the need for the law to have 'integrity' or 'fairness' but little about the law's authority. Although the integrity or fairness of the law is vital so is the law's authority. If Dworkin had stepped back from the lawyer's perspective he might have seen this point.

The institutional perspective stands back from the lawyer's perspective, not in order to disregard it, but to examine lawyers and courts in the wider perspective of their place in the social organisation and political institutions of a society.

The 'institutional' perspective has had many representatives in the history of legal philosophy. Its influence started with Thomas Hobbes in 'Leviathan' (1651) who heavily influenced Bentham ('Of Laws in General' (1782)) and Austin ('The Province of Jurisprudence Determined' (1832)). Hobbes placed law in its wider political context. Hobbes argued that strong authority was needed to pacify a society for without a common authority to keep men 'in awe' the natural tendency of man was to war with his fellow men. Once the strong authority, the 'Leviathan' (from the Book of Job, Old Testament, Leviathan meaning a great sea beast; Chapter 41: 'Canst thou draw out Leviathan with an hook?' – so the State by analogy as something which should be overwhelmingly powerful and awe inspiring to people) was established then the laws were the commands of the sovereign authority designed to maintain civil peace. Hobbes thus provided an account of law in terms of political and social needs. Austin and Bentham continued this tradition. Austin and Bentham first of all identified the sovereign in a society by considering 'habits of obedience' in that society and then in the tradition of Thomas Hobbes, identifying law as the 'commands of the sovereign'. If Austin and Bentham's account of law is too 'thin', ie lacks explanatory power, it is not because of the 'institutional' perspective they adopted with regard to law but because the terms they employed in their description of law – 'sovereign', 'habits of obedience', 'sanctions', 'commands' were too few in number and too simplistic to give an adequate descriptive analysis of law and legal systems.

Austin and Bentham explained the nature of the political system and then proceeded to explain the nature of law by placing it within the political system. H.L.A. Hart continued that 'institutional' tradition by examining law against the context of social and political needs. For example Hart has a famous 'fable' in 'The Concept of Law' (1961) to show the general social benefits a system of law might bring to a society governed by social rules only. Those benefits include the ability to change rules quickly through Parliamentary amendment and procedures to determine the exact scope of a social rule through the setting up of a court structure. Hart also shows how different legal rules help to plan social life out of court through laws on contract, marriages and wills for example. Hart's approach is to show how the institution of law cannot be understood without considering law against the background of the social and political matrix that the law operates in. Therefore the 'lawyer's perspective' on law, although valuable for some purposes, is arbitrary as the ultimate viewpoint on law if not for the simple fact that law is a social institution.

With regard to the 'institutional perspective' it is important to make a further sub-division between legal philosophers. There is (a) the 'engaged' institutional perspective and (b) the detached or 'disengaged' perspective.

The 'engaged' institutional perspective is the viewpoint of the legal theorist who seeks to give an account of law from the wide institutional perspective, placing law in its wider political and social context but who has some sort of commitment to or endorsement of a particular legal system or type of legal system. Examples of this type of approach are John Finnis in 'Natural Law and Natural Rights' (1980), Dennis Galligan in 'Law in Modern Society' (2007) and Neil MacCormick in 'Institutions of Law' (2007). Finnis regards 'the central case' of law as being a rationally prescribed ordering by those in authority for the common good of that community. Finnis uses this ideal of law ('ideal' because given human limitations it is not fully realisable) as a standard or a lens through which to examine actual legal systems. Indeed Finnis would say that an adequate account of modern western democratic legal systems (which generally seek to work for the common good) is not possible unless the theorist attends to the moral reasons which cause such legal systems to come into being and be sustained. In an essay entitled 'The Truth in Legal Positivism' (in *The Autonomy of Law*, edited by Robert George) Finnis argues:

> 'the reasons people have for establishing systems of positive law and for maintaining them include certain moral reasons, on which many of those people often act. And only those moral reasons suffice to explain why such people's undertaking takes the shape it does, giving legal systems the many defining features they have'.

Therefore for Finnis although he adopts the 'institutional perspective' seeking to examine law in its wider social context he does so with a commitment to an ideal form of law ('an ordering of reason for the common good' – the definition of law provided by the father of natural law theory: St. Thomas Aquinas in the 13th century) and a commitment to the western style of democratic government under the rule of law which at least tries to govern for the common good.

In a slightly different way Dennis Galligan has a strong commitment to a certain type of law, not an 'ideal' type favoured by Finnis but the few societies in the existing world which have what Galligan calls 'modern legal orders'. As Galligan says, such praiseworthy legal systems are few in number – the societies of Western Europe, north America, parts of the British Commonwealth and occasionally elsewhere. Galligan gives a full descriptive account of such legal systems in 'Law in Modern Society' (2007). Such societies are governed by a rule of law which is taken seriously by government and there is also a 'bond of trust' between legal officials such as police, judges, etc. and the public which is a defining mark of such modern legal orders and is absent in the corruption soaked officialdom of the rest of the world. Galligan makes it clear in his concluding paragraph that he is writing the book to further the protection of modern legal orders. Galligan writes:

> 'Legal orders with the features charted and discussed here are of interest and importance compared with other types of legal orders, not for reasons of western truimphalism, but because they have been

effective in producing social goods that are valued in western societies and beyond. They are at the same time fragile and unstable, so that if they are to be sustained they must first be understood.'

Neil MacCormick in 'Institutions of Law' (2007) focuses on constitutional law-states (Rechstaat in German) and MacCormick is himself committed in his description to the basic values of those 'institutional normative orders' as MaCormick calls them. MacCormick seeks to uphold the values of those 'law-States' few in number in the world, which are dedicated to the values of realising peace, justice and the common good under the rule of law. MacCormick's enterprise thus resembles Galligan's to decsribe the features of a small number of constitutional law states whilst being wholly committed to the values those few law states uphold.

There is certainly a place in legal theory for the sort of standpoint that Finnis, MaCormick and Galligan occupy but it should not be the ultimate standpoint of the legal theorist. This is where the third standpoint comes into play – the detached 'institutional' or 'external' perspective.

William Twining notes in 'Institutions of Law from a Global Perspective' (in *Law as Institutional Normative Order*, edited by Del Mar and Bankowski, 2009) that:

'pluaralism of beliefs and ideologies is a fact and that legal phenomena are immensely varied and complicated'

and as such the legal theorist if he wants to achieve great generality in his account of law and legal systems should not get engaged to or committed with a particular type of legal system. Professor Hart in *The Concept of Law* aimed to develop a descriptive theory of law involving the standpoint of an external juristic observer taking into account the 'internal point of view' of participants in a legal system but not claiming to be approving of or engaged with any particular legal system. Hart's external or institutional 'detached' perspective is the most appropriate for an explanation of all legal systems whether those legal systems are wicked, weak, corrupt, inefficient, incoherent, unjust or just plain indifferent.

For many, Hart's detached perspective will be the correct one to adopt if the observer is a sociologist, a comparative lawyer, an empirical researcher, a historian or if the politics of the observer are anarchistic in outlook. It should always be remembered that even in the most benign constitutional law state, law is a product of other people's power and this insight should caution against too ready an endorsement of any legal system.

Hart is sometimes accused of actually endorsing law whilst at the same time pretending to maintain a detachment from law. The problem arises because of Hart's use of a story to describe the move from a pre-legal society to a society with law and the benefits that might bring. Some have suggested (eg Roger Cotterrell in 'The Politics of Jurisprudence' 2003) that Hart is endorsing and encouraging some version of the rule of law for all societies. This view of Hart is a mistake. John Gardner explains in a 2010 Research paper 'Hart on Legality, Justice and Morality':

'In Chapter 5 of "The Concept of Law" Hart tells his brilliant and seminal fable of the emergence of a legal system (differentiated by its secondary rules of recognition, adjudication, and change) from an imagined pre-legal or proto legal arrangement of customary primary rules alone. As a way of making such a development rationally intelligible, his narrative emphasises the gains in efficiency and predictability that these secondary norms bring with them. Unfortunately, to the lasting confusion of many readers, he thereby makes it sound like he is extolling the virtues of the transformation from proto-law to law. Not surprisingly, he is, therefore taken to task by some critics for attempting to smuggle in a political ideology under cover of his supposedly ideology-neutral explanation of the nature of law. And that political ideology seems to many, not implausibly, to be none other than the ideology of the rule of law. . . . For all its brilliance, then, Hart's fable is afflicted by severe and damaging presentational flaws. The secondary rules, Hart should have clear, do not automatically bring with them the rule of law and, even for believers in the rule of law, their arrival is not necessarily to be welcomed. For life without any law at all might well be better than life with law but without the rule of law. The arrival of a legal system makes some forms of oppression possible, and others easier, and there is a further step to be taken to help protect against such law-enabled and law-facilitated oppression, namely the step from having a legal system to having a legal system under the rule of law.'

Hart was well aware of the costs as well as the benefits of law to a society. In a key passage for understanding Hart in *The Concept of Law*, Hart comments on the dangers of law

'the cost is the risk that the centrally organized power may well be used for the oppression of numbers with whose support it can dispense, in a way that the simpler regime of primary rules could not.'

Hart's stance towards law was thus one of detachment, aware of the benefits law could bring a society but also aware of how law allowed the more efficient and organised oppression of the population. In other words, for Hart law was 'morally risky' and scholastic detachment was the correct intellectual response. Hart maintained in the 'Postscript' to the second edition of *The Concept of Law* that it was futile to look for any purpose for law beyond guiding conduct. MacCormick, in 'Why Law Makes No Claims' (in *Law, Rights and Discourse*, edited by Pavlakos), claims that:

> 'Law is for the securing of civil peace so far as possible'

This Thomas Hobbes inspired insight into law's function by MacCormick would perhaps have been too strong for Professor Hart who would go no further with any 'inherent' purpose or function of law than to declare in the 'Postscript' to the second edition of *The Concept of Law* (1994):

> 'my theory makes no claim to identify the point or purpose of law or legal practices as such ... I think it quite vain to seek any more specific purpose which law serves beyond providing guides to human conduct and standards of criticism of such conduct.'

AIM HIGHER

Students can gain extra marks by locating the perspective on law that a particular legal theorist takes. Is the theorist describing law from the perspective of an ideal form of law, or describing law in neutrally descriptive terms or is the theorist praising in his description of legal systems a particular form of legal ordering such as modern western legal orders?

Notes

The best account on 'perspectives in legal theory' is Professor Raz's essay 'The Nature of Law' in *Ethics in the Public Domain* (1994). Professor Hart's account of his own 'general and descriptive' methodology in legal theory can be found in the 'Postscript' of the second edition to *The Concept of Law* (1994) especially at pp 239–241 and pp 248–249. Professor Finnis's legal methodology can be discerned in Chapter 1 of *Natural Law and Natural Rights* (1980). D. Galligan's 'engaged' description of modern legal orders can be found in 'Law in Modern Society' (2007) and Neil MacCormick's 'engaged' description of modern constitutional 'law-states' can be found in 'Institutions of Law' (2007).

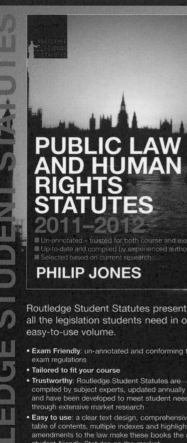